# MIXED/OTHER

# MIXED/OTHER

## Explorations of Multiraciality in Modern Britain

## Natalie Morris

First published in Great Britain in 2021 by Trapeze
an imprint of The Orion Publishing Group Ltd
Carmelite House, 50 Victoria Embankment,
London EC4Y 0DZ

An Hachette UK company

1 3 5 7 9 10 8 6 4 2

A CIP catalogue record for this book is
available from the British Library.

ISBN (Hardback): 978 1 409 19714 0
ISBN (eBook): 978 1 409 19716 4

Typeset by Born Group

Printed and bound in Great Britain by Clays Ltd, Elcograf S.p.A.

MIX
Paper from
responsible sources
FSC® C104740

www.orionbooks.co.uk

For Dad
Always, always

# Contents

# A note on terminology . . .

Before we get into this, I want to at least attempt to address some of the awkward imperfections that arise when talking and writing about race. The words we use to talk about ideas of race and ethnicity are important, meaningful and often deeply personal, which means it is damn near impossible to objectively decide on terminology that is going to feel right for every-body. This is especially the case when talking about those of mixed ethnicity. Similarly, these terms shouldn't be conflated. Race refers to the socially ascribed categories distinguished by specific physical traits such as skin colour, whereas ethnicity is a broader term that also includes cultural characteristics such as language, ancestry, traditions and beliefs. I use both terms at different points throughout the book, but they don't mean the same thing.

As a society, at the time during which I am writing this book, we haven't yet landed on a universally agreed way to talk about race, or to describe mixed ethnicity, and this may never happen. Language is something that is constantly shifting and evolving and is often fixed to the time in which you are living. 'Coloured', for example, was widely accepted terminology for my grandparents' generation. It's quite likely, then, that when I'm a grandma, the terminology I have used in this book will feel wildly outdated.

However, this is more than a disclaimer for my future self, a get-out-of-jail card to save an older version of me some possible embarrassment. The words I choose to use in this book matter today – now. There are strong and divergent opinions within *this* generation about which words should be used when discussing mixed heritage, and which words are not appropriate, and it therefore wouldn't feel right wading into this discussion without a brief explanation of the thought process behind my choice of language.

As you will have guessed from these first few paragraphs, and the title of the book, I'm cool with the use of the term 'mixed'. It's how I describe myself – in my eyes I'm a Black, mixed woman – and it is the terminology I am most comfortable using about myself and others with multiple ethnic heritage. It also seems to be the most popular terminology among the different people I interviewed for this book, although I am aware that many of those people are of the same generation as me, which likely has an impact on our collective preference.

I'll briefly lay out why I stuck with 'mixed' over some of the other possible descriptors that I considered. First, biracial: this term is too limited for what I am exploring in this book, as some people who are mixed have more than two different ethnicities in their heritage. Next, multiracial: this covers the different possible groups, but I want to avoid language that overtly uses 'race' as part of the description. Dual heritage again has limits in focusing on duality. Multiheritage: this is definitely a viable alternative option, but my unfamiliarity with the term and the fact that it isn't commonly used in the UK discouraged me.

So, I'm going with 'mixed'. I'm consciously avoiding using the term 'mixed race', and this is a new thing for me. I described myself as 'mixed race' for most of my life. Even as recently as a year or two ago, I wouldn't have seen a problem with the term, which proves again how we are constantly shifting and adapting our opinions and understandings of language, and the connotations of certain words. Now, I find 'mixed race' a more problematic descriptor because I think it reinforces the idea of race as something essential or biological. Using 'mixed' on its own is my very small way of attempting to limit and disrupt our reliance on archaic ideas about race.

Everything I write in this book is underpinned by the concept that race is a social construct, rather than a biological fact. This theory, now widely recognised, is that there is no biological basis to our racial categories and that the things we use to create these different groups – from physical and aesthetic markers, to cultural customs and norms – are entirely social. That isn't to say that race isn't real; the implications of these racial categories are hugely important and impact everything from our relationships to our prospects for professional success, and even our life expectancy and how safe we feel in the world. Instead, this book is based on the belief that all of the implications of race are profoundly real, but there is no biological basis to the ways we divide and categorise ourselves in terms of race.

So I personally avoid using the term 'mixed race' as much as possible, but when it comes to the people I interviewed during my research for this book, I prefer them to use whichever terminology they are most comfortable with because I believe self-identification is important and gives people the freedom to speak about their own experiences with more conviction and authenticity.

It's a good thing that language changes and evolves over time, that mixed people are no longer referred to as 'half-castes' or 'mulattos' (at least not in polite company, anyway), and in ten years' time – or sooner – we may decide that 'mixed' no longer works. It's a good thing that we are constantly questioning and rigorously examining the words we use, changing our minds, admitting when we were wrong, interrogating our inner biases. That's how attitudes are changed, and how important conversations are started.

Language is not just about words. The words we choose to use convey meanings, and those meanings can inform the way people think. When those words are being used to describe minoritised groups of people, the meanings they convey need to be thought about. Careless use of language can be incredibly damaging, and the effects can reverberate through entire generations.

'Mixed' isn't the ideal solution to my terminology problem. Some argue that the word itself reinforces the idea of some kind of racial 'purity' in which different 'pure' categories can be combined like ice-cream flavours. I understand this criticism, and I don't really have a counter-argument other than to say that, despite this problem, this is the term that works best for me right now, and to acknowledge the fact that it won't work for everybody. Like I said, it's imperfect.

Come back to me in ten years and I might have a better answer. Or at the very least, I will have a different one.

# Introduction

# Where are you really from?

I will never fail to be shocked by how brazen people are when they ask me where I'm from – where I'm *really* from. The audacity is wild. Before they ask my name, or how I am, they want to know where my parents were born, how I identify; they want to know why they can't fit me into one of the neat categories they have in their head.

It's not the curiosity that I take issue with; I don't mind people asking questions and wanting to know more about me, it's the fact that it is so often the *first* thing people want to know. It's also the intention behind the question. When some people ask; 'Where are you *from* from?' they are asking from a place of common understanding, of looking for a connection. But for others, the question comes from a place of inherent discomfort. My face falls outside of the distinct tick-boxes that they recognise and understand, and they need me to immediately explain why.

If you're mixed, you've probably experienced this – the pressure to explain why you don't fit, why you look the way you do, why your family looks like it does. But we don't owe anyone an explanation, and certainly not strangers or people we barely know. We don't owe them any attempt to soothe their discomfort at not being able to place us. When they ask me where I'm from, I want to ask them why it matters, and what they really mean with that question. This question usually masks another question, something more unpleasant and dehumanising: 'What are you?'

What's strange about the frequency of this line of questioning is the fact that we are not exactly novel. There are loads of us. The number of Brits who identify as having a mixed background almost doubled between the census of 2001 and 2011, to about 1.2m – slightly more than two per cent of the overall population. Experts say this figure is likely to be an underestimate, as not all children of mixed relationships will have ticked one of the mixed categories; there may be a significant number who chose to tick the box they most closely identify with – Black or Asian – rather than 'mixed'. This trend of growth is also likely to have continued since the last census, so this percentage could be much higher by now.

Despite this rapidly growing population, what I learned over the course of my research for this book is that being mixed can so often be about searching. Searching for others like you. Searching for a solid sense of belonging. It can be isolating to be the only one in your family who looks like you do, the only one in your group of friends who experiences life through this specific lens of in-betweenness. When people are constantly demanding that you explain yourself, asking you to map out your genealogy within minutes of meeting you, it only reinforces this sense of otherness.

When I was born, there was no official way for my parents to record my ethnicity accurately on the census. There was no category for 'mixed' until 2001; before that the only options were: 'Black-Other' and 'Any other ethnic group'. My parents can't remember which box they ticked on my behalf. An entire mixed generation grew up watching the world define and categorise our identity in real-time.

Tick-boxes and restrictive labels are certainly not the be-all and end-all, and I didn't spend the first decade of my life with any awareness of my official lack of categorisation, or any great longing for a tick-box all of my own. But the fact that even during the three decades of my relatively short life-time, I have already seen a significant evolution in the way the mixed population is perceived and recognised in society, shows how far we still have to go. We are still so early in our journey of understanding mixedness and placing it within wider discussions about ethnicity. It's vital that we find better, more inclusive ways to communicate these ideas. Maybe then people will stop demanding we tell them where we're *really* from' with such regularity, or at least without the assumption that they are entitled to an explanation from us.

For me, belonging has always been about so much more than a simple definition of my ethnicity; an easy equation that combines my parents' heritage to tell me where I fit. Belonging is something you feel, under your skin, as you move through the world. It is fluid and utterly dependent on context – where you are, when you are, who you're with, who's perceiving you. It's something that is so big, so vital, so abstract, that it can't be flattened or contained in tick-box form.

If you're reading this, I can assume that your motives are more inquisitive than hostile, so you can have my answer to the 'where are you *really* from?' question, in brief. My mother, Kim, is white British. She grew up in Staffordshire with her parents and two younger siblings. She met my father, they had me and my sister, then moved to Manchester to raise us. Mum did the day-to-day parenting on her own after they divorced when I was seven, and my sister and I are both incredibly close to her. I owe her everything. My dad's parents are Jamaican, but he was born in London after they came over in the late 1950s as part of the Windrush Generation. My dad, Tony, was brought up in the care system in Portsmouth. His foster mother was a white woman called Audrey and he loved her. He lived with Audrey from the age of six months and stayed there until he joined the RAF at 16. His biological parents were on the peripheries of his life, but they never brought him home to live with them. Dad is my inspiration, the reason I do what I do. He became ill very suddenly and died on 1 August 2020, shattering my heart.

My understanding of belonging begins with them. Not their ethnicity, or how they look, or the fact that I am intrinsically different to both of them, though my face is an undeniable blend of the two of theirs. It's more the feeling I get when I'm with them, when I think about them – the feeling of home; and my sister, Becky, too, who is the younger, louder, more brilliant version of myself. Our little unit is the only tick-box I need to feel part of something.

Where do I belong? I am sitting on Dad's shoulders watching a sea of writhing bodies dressed in feathers and sequins, neon crop tops and body paint, Afros bouncing and intricate braids whipping, beads of sweat like dew drops on dark skin, and I feel the bass climbing up through the pavement, snaking through Dad's body and into my own. He has one hand locked on my ankle; the other is gripping Becky's hand tightly as we cascade with the crowd from the top of the hill, just outside the tube station, into the mass of rippling colour and sound below.

Dad loved taking us to Carnival when we were little. We had been to Manchester Carnival a few times, but this was the first time we had been to Notting Hill, and I had never seen anything like it. I dug my fingers into Dad's head as we swayed down the hill, the air shrill with whistles that cut through something deeper and heavier, which clattered my heart against my ribs.

It was hot in the way you only get down south, in a way that I had only experienced before when on holiday. It was the thick, treacly closeness of late summer in the mid-nineties, not the washout, almost autumnal August bank holiday week-ends we tend to get now. Dad set me down and I tied my sweatshirt around my waist, freeing my arms, feeling the sun's heat press against my skin. Underneath I was wearing a bright blue crop top from Tammy Girl that made me feel powerful. Becky and I ate chicken charred from the grill with dense dumplings, Dad ate something spicier and drank something sweet and red that we weren't allowed to try. He pointed out the different flags that people were waving or wearing, and I tried to make a mental note of every Jamaican flag I saw: our flag.

We settled in front of a sound system with lots of families who looked like us, lots of dads like our dad. Enough space around us to move, to breathe. I didn't know the music, but I could close my eyes and feel it in my body like a second heartbeat, dictating a new rhythm for my blood. Dad started dancing and Becky and I sprang into action beside him, at his ankles, swaying and wiggling, laughing hysterically. Later, we danced behind a float as it crawled forward. They were playing hip hop, tunes we played at home, and Becky and I knew what to do, how to move. I looked up at Dad and he had lost himself in the music, eyes closed, head nodding, both hands in the air. He opened his eyes and smiled at me and I felt impossibly grown up dancing next to him. I grabbed Becky's tiny hand in mine, and we jumped on the spot until we were exhausted. Later, Dad scooped us up and waded back towards the tube station, to Euston, to home. It isn't possible to feel as though you don't belong when you have memories like this one.

For me, belonging is a multitude of feelings. It is the warmth and security that I feel when I am with the people in my life who love me, who know me, who accept me. I belong with both sides of my family; I belong to different communities and regions; I belong with my friends, with my boyfriend. Belonging is not solely attached to ethnicity, and for mixed people, a sense of belonging can be found – or created – in unexpected places.

There is no one singular story of mixedness, no one tidily explained experience that can convey the multiplicities of how we feel, how we see ourselves. The stories of my life as a Black mixed woman in Britain – from my first carnival, to my first box braids, from being called 'mongrel' by a Black man, to being called 'nigger' by a white man – are just a drop in the vast complexities of mixedness, the unique, varied, incomparable experiences that make us who we are.

I can only speak of being mixed in the way that *I* am mixed, in the specific time and place that *I* exist. To get a fuller, more nuanced picture of multiraciality in modern Britain, we have to open up the conversation. We have to hear from people with alternative backgrounds, different perspectives, the voices that are frequently forgotten, people who reflect the many different narratives that exist within mixedness. This is the only way to move beyond the concept that 'mixed' is a homogenous group, that we all experience the world in the same way, when the reality is that this couldn't be further from the truth.

The mainstream conversation around mixedness is stilted, repetitive and often problematic. We are repeatedly presented as lost souls, caught between two worlds, adrift in a sea of rejection, not enough of one thing, not enough of another. We're told that to be mixed is to be confused, muddled, unsure of who we are. On the other side of that spectrum, we're treated as a trend. Our physical features are Instagrammable, covetable, plastered on billboards and adverts. White women openly share their desire for mixed babies, as though skin tone, curl pattern and eye colour are things they will be able to choose like cinema pick 'n' mix.

When we *are* given a voice, rather than simply dissected for our 'desirable' parts, the analysis rarely goes beyond questions of identity and belonging. While these are important and valuable conversations to have, they are not enough in isolation. We need context for these discussions to have real meaning. We need to make sure we're not skirting over the awkward, more difficult parts.

Too often, the trickier elements of the conversation are carefully stepped around or ignored altogether. How do we navigate the privileges that come with being mixed, the proximity to whiteness that opens so many doors? How do we recognise the internalised racism or anti-Blackness that can be upheld by mixed individuals and mixed families? What part do we play in the perpetuation of colourism? How do we reconcile our privilege with the mistrust, disapproval and microaggressions that we also have to bear? How do we ensure that conversations about mixedness aren't centred around whiteness, that those who are mixed without white heritage are not sidelined or excluded? Does advocating for a mixed identity equate to a rejection of your minority heritage?

These are the tough questions, the uncomfortable questions. But to have any real grasp on the complexity of what it means to be mixed in modern Britain, we need to confront them.

xix

This is so much deeper than black and white. This is about the infinite shades in between, the different elements that blend and entwine to a point where they are impossible to separate. To talk about mixedness in any meaningful way requires us to move beyond binary thinking about race – that you have to be one thing or another. The mixed population is not one thing or the other, we are neither and both, and we want the freedom to exist in these spaces without scrutiny or suspicion.

I'm writing this book not as an academic, a sociologist or a race theorist. I'm a journalist, a writer, a storyteller, and this book will bring you my story of personal exploration, the memories and moments that make up my experience of being mixed in modern Britain. But my perspective is nowhere near enough to comprehensively represent what it means to be mixed today, so I will also bring other people's stories to life. Stories from people from different walks of life, from different parts of the country, with different perspectives. They are stories of hope and loss, joy and understanding, and while everyone I've spoken to has a unique story to tell, at the heart of all of them is a thread of common connection, a relatable wave trickling through each narrative that will make you nod your head in recognition, whether you're mixed yourself, or you have mixed family members, friends or colleagues.

We hear Anna's story, her struggles with passing as white, her deep connection with her Japanese heritage, and the guilt she feels when she sees her mother experiencing overt racism. Luke explains how he has grappled with his identity over the years, how he eventually became comfortable with the 'mixed' label after initially pushing back against it. Bilal outlines the microaggressions he faced at Cambridge – from his first interaction with a white student who assumed he was selling drugs – and shares how he has felt excluded from the mixed narrative because he doesn't have a white parent. Joseph talks of growing up in the 1970s, the overt racism and violence he had to live with, and his solo pilgrimage to find his estranged father in a remote Nigerian village.

During more than a year of research, interviews, and deeper than deep conversations, it has become abundantly clear that there are some commonalities in the mixed experience that transcend the differences between us. These are the feelings, the specific lived moments, the complicated contradictions, which people shared with me, again and again, regardless of their specific mix of ethnicities. Through an exploration of these common themes, the areas of our lives in which our racial identity seems to affect us the most, I take a look at how our perspectives unite us, and how our individual experiences of mixedness are unique for each one of us.

In many ways, this is a book about belonging. It is about finding a place where you fit, where the people around you have an inherent understanding of how you see the world and how you see yourself. It is about finding that nod of acknowledgement, that half smile of recognition that says, 'You're the same as me.' At the same time, it is so much more than that.

It's vital that throughout these discussions we keep in mind the reality that 'race' is a social construct, and what we are analysing are the real effects these constructs continue to have on the lives of minoritised, racialised and mixed individuals. This book is about reimagining how we talk about multiraciality, dissecting how we perceive and understand mixedness, and ultimately reframing the discussion into something more nuanced, more considered, and more reflective of the lived experiences of the mixed population in Britain today. Our stories are at the heart of that. We find strength in the narratives that tie us together, but there is also a real power in our individuality.

# Chapter 1

# Identity

Figuring out your identity is to ask the question, 'Who am I?' It's a big question; an impossibly enormous question. To distil the reams of experiences, opinions, beliefs, behaviours and attitudes that make up a person into an easily digestible sentence – or even a chapter in a book – seems hopelessly simplistic. But we do it all the time. We love reducing people to a single, overarching characteristic that defines who they are because that is much, much simpler than delving into the messy, contradictory realities of what it means to be a human being.

I do it all the time. Who am I? I am a woman. A cisgenderheterosexual woman. A mixed woman. A Black woman. A sister, a daughter, a writer. A netball player, a movie addict, a lover of cheese, a cat person. A Mancunian. I'm competitive, sensitive, impatient, hard-working, caring. These are the labels I use, the elements of myself I choose to focus on vary depending on the context; who I'm with, where I am, what I'm trying to convey about myself at any given point.

Do these descriptions sum me up adequately? To me, they feel thin, like a watered-down, half-dissolved version of who I understand myself to be. But articulating identity is inevitably going to be limiting because who you are, who you are *really*, tends to transcend language and settle itself, ungraspable, in the warm, hidden place behind your heart, in the way your smile flashes up to your eyes, the secret memories you think about before you fall asleep, the small ways you give and accept love. But still, we strive to put it into words; to boil ourselves down to some essential, concentrated form of 'self'.

Identity is the constellation of a person. Shining points in the darkness which, when connected, map out a rough outline of who you are. These individual spots of light that we pick out to tell a story about ourselves can be so many different things; from the way we dress, to the car we drive, the football team we support, to the music we listen to, our profession, to our place in our family or friendship group. Defining your identity is a way of aligning yourself with others who identify in the same way as you do. The constellations become galaxies, solar systems, of interconnectivity; it is as much about the collective as it is about the individual. This is why identity can be such a sticky issue for mixed people. The way in which society constructs racial categories makes those natural, collective alignments harder to pick out.

Race is just one of our identities, one of the many ways we can define ourselves, but it's an important and inescapable one. As long as the world we live in perpetuates a damaging racial hierarchy that creates real and systemic inequalities, racial identity will continue to be an intrinsic element of self for all of us. It doesn't matter that race is a social construction with no biological basis; the real-life effects of race are real. How you define yourself and how society defines you in terms of race has major implications for how you move through the world, your chances of success, your safety, and being positioned as a minority makes the need to belong to a group all the more pertinent. But what happens to your sense of self when even the minority groups don't completely align with who you think you are?

I think about my identity when I look in the mirror. I see my dad's face staring back at me. The large forehead (we are fully paid-up members of the fivehead gang), the crooked bottom teeth, the full bottom lip, something in my eyes is his as well. My height and the sport-honed leanness of my body. All Dad. As I get older, I am starting to look more like my mum. The bulbous ball of flesh at the tip of my nose, the arch of my eyebrows, the way my eyes crinkle into nothing when I laugh.

I came across an old photograph of my mum, younger than I am now, before she was my mum, when she was just Kim. She's at Notting Hill Carnival, a pilgrimage she and Dad would make from the Midlands every summer, before my sister and I arrived. In the picture she is a walking emblem of the late 1980s. She wears a simple, bottle green T-shirt, chunky sunglasses hang from a chain around her neck, enormous gold earrings dangle beneath a voluminous, chestnut-coloured perm, pinned at the top to create more height than you might think possible for a white woman's hair. Her eyes are closed, and she is necking a giant beer like a trooper. She is glowing, she is living her best life, and her face looks exactly like mine. The face shape, the cheekbones – it's like looking into a mirror.

It's both uncanny and incredibly gratifying at the same time. It makes me feel proud to see myself in her. Seeing my own face transplanted in this way tethers me to the earth in some solid sense. It is a physical trace of my identity at a different point in time, a time before I even existed. It is both soothing and legitimising. I belong here. I have history here.

My mum is white and I am not. While that has had absolutely no impact on our relationship, nor has it impeded our ability to become incredibly close, it does mean that as much as I am growing to see my own face in the face of my mother, the rest of the world does not, or will not, see that. There is some inherent barrier of perception. Because, while I am allowed to be Black like my dad, I am definitely not allowed to be white. Whiteness has never been something I have aspired to, but feeling physically 'othered' from one of your own parents, even as you slowly morph into them, is a tricky emotion to navigate. It hacks away at my tether, at the connecting points in my personal history.

The shock that some people express when they find out that my mum is my mum, the instant assumption that we couldn't possibly be related, makes me feel as though my identity lies in the hands of others; as though other people can determine, just by looking at me, where I do not belong. It happens all the time. I've been told by a million different people, in a million different ways, what I am and what I am not, and it is maddening. From a friend telling me that I 'actually look Black' when I got box braids for the first time, to a colleague asking me to put together an 'urban' playlist for a work event because 'you'll know about these things', to being sent private messages on Instagram asking me how I have the audacity to write about racism when I'm 'not Black'.

I know who I am. I am a mixed woman. I am a Black woman. So any uncertainty or confusion isn't coming from me. The only time problems ever arise is when other people decide they have a better idea of who I am than I do, and feel entitled to just jump right in and tell me. It's frustrating and it can feel uniquely isolating too. I want to get to a point where I can feel confident in asserting my identity without having that assertion immediately undermined or questioned. That's how you allow people to feel secure in who they are; that's how true acceptance is cultivated.

Luke is a twenty-six-year-old poet from Sussex of Jamaican and British heritage, and in the last few years he has realised that his desire to identify as mixed is, in part, about filling a hole. He feels that something has been missing for him and redefining his identity in terms of ethnicity helps to give his existence purpose. He says this lack of direction is a generational feeling.

'The purpose of a person used to be religion, or it was family, there might be a war, or certain political movements like capitalism or communism,' says Luke. 'Now we get to my generation, and everything feels quite purposeless.'

Luke has a day job too; he works in advertising, but it is poetry where his skills and passion truly lie. He ascribes the purposelessness that he feels to a drastic shift in the domestic sphere. People of Luke's age aren't really getting married any more, more people are choosing not to have children or can't afford to, owning property in a major city is basically a myth, and stable, linear careers are largely a thing of the past. How do we create meaning for ourselves in the absence of these traditional markers of progress, direction and success? I'm a few years older than Luke, but I can relate to these existential anxieties; I feel them acutely. Luke says our individual identities feel like a good place to start.

'A lot of people in my circles attach themselves to climate change to find that direction,' explains Luke. 'For me, my mixed-race identity has been the thing to give me that sense of purpose.

'Identifying in this way helps me to answer the question "Who am I?" It isn't a complete answer, and my thoughts on this change quite frequently. I still have a lot of things that I'm trying to work out and understand, but I think that confusion is a good thing. Confusion means you're at least trying to figure it out.'

Identity is something we all create in an attempt to make sense of the world around us. But just because we have created them, or because they have a social basis rather than a biological one, doesn't mean our identities don't have real implications for how we move through the world. As Luke has discovered, calling yourself one thing, another thing, or a mix of things, can affect how other people see you, and how you see yourself.

For mixed people, the answer to the question 'Who am I?' is often taken out of our hands. The designation of who we are becomes the prerogative of everyone we meet and is subject to dissection based on ideas about singular racial categories. Not only is the question taken away, but it is often morphed into something more dehumanising. Not, 'Who are you?' but, '*What* are you?' It is a question that most mixed people will have encountered either directly or indirectly at some point. But whether posed bluntly, or more delicately ('Where are you *from*, from?'), it is a question that can betray a deep discomfort with an identity that isn't easily or neatly defined.

It is this projection that makes mixed identity so slippery. When who you are is dependent upon how others see you in any given situation, it can be destabilising, especially if the label given to you is incongruous with how you see your-self. It's also important to acknowledge that not every mixed person will experience this, and it would definitely be wrong to assume that there is anything inherent about being mixed that leads to some kind of internal crisis.

There is a tired stereotype that says to be mixed is to be in a permanent state of uncertainty and confusion around your identity, rejected by both sides of your heritage, confused and conflicted about who you are in some integral, irrevocable way that causes damage to your life. It's an old trope but a persistent one. One in three parents of young children thinks there is the potential for a child to become confused if they have parents from different racial or ethnic backgrounds,[1] but my research shows that this is not the case at all.

I've interviewed more than fifty mixed people over the last year and the overwhelming majority had a strong sense of who they are and how they wanted to identify. Although we have to consider the fact that people who volunteer to talk to a writer about their identity in terms of their ethnicity may be more likely to have solid personal perspectives on the subject, it does seem as though the real conflict comes from the external; from a societal need to explain the existence of a person in a way that doesn't ring true with their experience of the world. It's a damaging by-product of a society that is doggedly determined to reiterate monoraciality as the norm. Mixed people may feel isolated at times, but again, that is a result of limiting, binary thinking about race. To say we are collectively experiencing a crisis of identity feels more like a projection of the discomfort felt by others at the thought of dual or fluid existence.

This sense of an identity crisis plays into one of the most archaic, insulting narratives about mixed people: the 'tragic mulatto' myth. The story depicts a mixed individual – usually a woman – who is inherently miserable, even suicidal, because of her inability to fit into a single racial category. We see these figures pop up again and again in novels and films throughout the twentieth century, and these mixed characters are almost always depicted as exclusively Black and white. In these narratives, the woman's entire life is torn apart through the discovery of her Black heritage, which she was desperately trying to conceal.

---

1   Caballero, Edwards and Puthussery, 'Parenting "Mixed" Children: Negotiating Difference and Belonging in Mixed Race, Ethnicity and Faith Families: Typifications of Difference and Belonging', Joseph Rowntree Foundation, 1st January 2008

She is depicted as unworthy, unlovable, pitiable, for no reason other than her mixed heritage. That's how she sees herself, too; the self-loathing is *real*. Historical context helps you understand these characters a bit better; these people were mixed African Americans who would choose to 'pass' as white if they could in order to access better jobs, education and live in an overtly racist society still deeply tainted by the legacies of slavery.

We will come back to the concept of 'passing' in greater detail in Chapter 6, but for now it is important to note that the message of these tales serves to prop up white superiority. They imply that there is something inherently deviant about racial mixing; that mixed offspring will be doomed to a life of shame, stigma and pain. The legacy of these stories is enduring and they are still being told today. Brit Bennett's bestselling 2020 novel *The Vanishing Half* is based on this theme, and Nella Larsen's 1929 novel *Passing* is being made into a new film for 2021. Despite the importance of recognising this period of modern history, these stories can perpetuate the mistaken belief that mixed people always want to hide or deny a part of themselves.

In light of the current cultural reverie for racial ambiguity and the recently established 'coolness' associated with being mixed, stories like this may not seem important now, but like all racial stereotypes, the damaging impact of these negative generalisations perseveres for generations. These old ideas have contributed to a notable minority of people today being uncomfortable with relationships across racial boundaries, and it leads them to justify this position with 'concern' for the child that may come of such a relationship.[2]

---

2 Childs, 'Listening to the Interracial Canary: Contemporary Views on Interracial Relationships Among Blacks and Whites', Fordham Law Review, Vol. 76, Issue 6, January 2008

This idea of 'crisis' may also come from the fact that there is so much variation in the way that mixed people choose to identify. Some identify as a single ethnicity, others prefer mixed, multi-heritage, or biracial, and for some it depends entirely on the context and where they are at any given point in their life. Personal identity is also affected by gender, class and location, and therefore any cross-section of the mixed population in Britain will likely describe themselves in many different ways. This lack of an overarching consensus may lead people to wrongly believe that to be mixed is to be in an identity crisis, but really it just means that people with multiracial heritage have many different ideas about how to describe themselves, and where they fit in the world. How can anyone expect us all to identify in the same way regardless of our own individual set of life circumstances?

A 2015 review of research on multiracial identity explained that 'discrimination toward out-group members drives in-group identification; however, multiracials do not have just one in-group – not all multiracials identify as multiracial, and their in-group identification may fluctuate over time.'[3] In other words, racial identity is, in part, based on concepts of 'us' versus 'them'. But when you're mixed, 'us' isn't a solid, singular or permanent category.

The review proposed that research on mixed identity needs to move away from monoracial concepts because 'it is clear that not only for the multiracial population but for anyone with multiple social identities (e.g., race, gender, age, occupation . . .), context can greatly sway how a person chooses to identify.'

---

3  Gaither, '"Mixed" Results: Multiracial Research and Identity Explorations', Current Directions in Psychological Science, Vol. 24, Issue 2, 6th April 6, 2015

The conversation about mixed identity needs to move beyond an analysis of 'crisis'. Not only is it tedious, it's also unhelpful. It bolsters binary thinking about race by implying that multiraciality has a negative impact on a person's emotional and psychological well-being, which strays danger-ously close to an understanding of race as something biological and essential, rather than a social construct. And, while it's important to acknowledge and understand the unique and varied difficulties that mixed people can face in a world that's geared towards monoraciality, it's also crucial to realise that conflict and struggle is far from the full picture of the multiracial experience.

The 2015 research review found that, 'multiracials have *identity flexibility*, or the ability to freely and easily switch between or identify with their multiple racial identities at a given moment.' Rather than crisis or confusion, the author concludes that this 'flexibility' grants mixed people the freedom of greater adaptability. And this is what people need to get their heads around. Nobody's identity is singular or fixed; regardless of ethnicity, who we are changes across the course of a lifetime. A flexible sense of self can be an incredible tool; an affirming, positive attribute that can actually strengthen your identity by widening your support systems, and there's nothing tragic about that.

Though it seems clear that mixed people are comfortable in being able to move between groups or identities, there can be a societal pressure to choose one or the other. Which one are you? Which are you more of? Which do you look more like? Which do you act more like? It is another symptom of a society that understands people in terms of singularity. If I tell someone I only identify as Black, it might make me slightly easier to place, easier to understand.

An American study found that one-in-five multiracial adults say they have felt pressure from friends, family or from society in general to choose one of the races in their background over another.[4] Those with Black heritage are likely to feel this more keenly, as are those who believe they physically look like a mix of races and not like just one race, suggesting that the greater your outward ambiguity, the more people will pressure you to explain yourself. But how you identify in terms of race is very rarely an individual choice. For mixed people it is so often dependent on external, social factors: how others see you, regardless of how you see yourself. So, this idea that mixed people get to pick which 'side' they identify with depending on how they feel is a fallacy.

I could never choose to be white, and the microaggressions and overt racism I have experienced at the hands of white people reinforces my otherness on a regular basis. At the same time, my proximity to whiteness and the privileges this grants me ensures that my experience of life is different to that of my Black family members. Neither definition is satisfactory for me, and neither 'side' comprehensively explains how I move through the world.

As I've said, I identify as Black and mixed. For me, it is possible and necessary to be both. What is difficult is the idea that to identify as mixed or biracial – or whatever terminology you prefer to use – is a *rejection* of one side or the other. Tiger Woods, whose mother is Thai, Chinese and Dutch, and father is African American, Chinese and Native American, refers to himself as 'Cablinasian' – an abbreviation made up of his parents' multiple heritages. Tiger has been

---

4   Parker, Horowitz, Morin and Lopez, 'Multiracial in America: Proud, Diverse and Growing in Numbers,' Pew Research Center, 11th June, 2015

repeatedly criticised for this assertion, with some saying that he is attempting to 'distance himself' from his Blackness[5]. It's not hard to work out why Tiger's comments on this subject have angered people in the past. Creating your own label to define your ethnicity is always going to rile some, and you can understand the frustration of those who want Tiger – the star of a sport that historically barred the participation of Black people – to present himself to the world as a Black man. The suggestion that by embracing multiplicity, Tiger Woods is *denying* a part of himself, though, is something that's hard to swallow.

The reaction to Tiger Woods' personalised racial category shows how much opposition mixed people can face when attempting to self-identify. It isn't realistic to assume that mixed people have the power or agency to effectively assert or deny anything about themselves because what we actually experience over and over again is society providing the labels for us. They tell us what we are, and when we try to tell them how we want to identify, they tell us we're wrong. Pick either 'side' and you will have your legitimacy questioned by someone. Pick neither 'side' and you're accused of rejection or self-hatred. So really, how is that a choice?

Back to Luke. He's Jamaican on his dad's side and white British on his mum's, but he has a pretty ambiguous look – he tells me that in certain spaces he is mistaken for Indian or Arab. Luke's direct experience tells him no matter how much you might want to pick a side, it just isn't possible. There will always be someone telling you what you can and can't be.

---

5   Davis W. Houck, 'Crouching Tiger, Hidden Blackness: Tiger Woods and the Disappearance of Race', Handbook of Sports and Media, Abingdon: Routledge, 17th April, 2006

'At one point in school, we had this old, white teacher and everyone found him funny,' said Luke, smiling wryly. 'He made grossly inappropriate jokes about every single thing. In the class there was only me and one other kid who wasn't white. This teacher went around the class and assigned nicknames. He called me "Black boy". He called other people, "big head", or "short guy", literally just aesthetic descriptions, which is definitely not OK nowadays.'

While Luke was in this class, he was literally being told – by someone in a position of power – that he was Black, and only Black. As Luke remembers it, he didn't feel comfortable with the teacher's behaviour, but there were inherent barriers stopping him from saying anything.

'There was this "banter" dynamic, so you couldn't take offence,' he explained.

When Luke was younger, he strongly identified as Black, which isn't surprising given that was how he was perceived by most of the people in his majority white education and neighbourhood growing up. He can even pinpoint the moment where his race first became apparent to him, the first time he really felt himself to be Black.

'It was learning about slavery in Year Five for the first time, and it was just such a weird experience. You go from this place where none of you see race and then suddenly – directly after this class – everyone sees race. That first lesson changes everything.' Luke spoke slowly and calmly, every word a deliberate choice – there was a precision in his choice of language that could only belong to a poet. But as he thought back to this moment, I felt his pace intensify.

'I remember reading the textbook and seeing this picture of a slave and just thinking, "What the fuck?" I looked up and everyone was just looking at me. I think I cried. I cried in the class. It felt like my world view was shattered in that moment.'

Luke told me that some time after this incident, a kid he had always hated called him 'chocolate bar' in the playground. Luke punched him – something that's quite difficult to imagine given his gentle tone of voice and demeanour. But it happened, and the school punished both of them.

Now Luke identifies as mixed, not Black. The decision largely came down to his analysis of other people's opinions of him; a personal realisation that 'Black' didn't quite define him adequately. As Luke got older, went to university, started mixing in more diverse circles, it became clear that his identity wasn't quite as cut-and-dry as he used to think.

'I was writing Black Panther quotes on my bedroom wall; I read Malcolm X's book when I was way too young to really understand it all. I felt that was who I was. So, then to be told that I wasn't Black – that was really destabilising for me. Everything completely changed.'

It was a girl who told Luke that he wasn't Black for the first time: 'She told me to stop code-switching,' says Luke. 'She said I was changing my accent depending on who I was with. She said: "Stop trying to speak like the man dem – you're not Black. Stick with your actual accent."'

In direct contradiction to his experience with the teacher, Luke was now being told in no uncertain terms that he was *not* Black. It made him re-evaluate his place in the world and how he saw himself. As jarring as it was to have his authenticity questioned in this way, he also felt that she might have a point.

'I mostly grew up with my white family. In a very white town. And I had certain privileges because of that, even if it was a challenge in some ways. So, I decided then that I can't really say that I'm Black. The Black experience is my dad's and my nan's experience, and I haven't shared that. By saying I'm Black, I'm essentially hijacking someone else's experience. I knew I needed to work out my own way.'

Luke uses his poetry as an outlet to work through his feelings and to organise his thoughts. His poem *Half-Stereotype* (which you can read in full at the end of this chapter) depicts his journey towards self-identification and the moments in his life that have defined who he is.

'I take ideas, convert them into metaphors and then I look at them. I ask myself: Why did I write these things? What do they mean to me? And then I break them down. Poetry is my reflection on myself. When I write a poem, I don't always agree with it the next year; they reflect a moment in time.' Luke becomes animated as he talks about his craft, his face lights up and I can suddenly imagine him on stage.

'One thing I talk about in my poem is the concept of being a different race to both of your parents:

"Looking into the eyes of your own mother
And realising that
You're not the same ethnicity as one another"

'I remember a conversation I had with my mum. She told me I should tell her if anyone at school said anything racist to me. She said: "Of course, I won't be able to understand the situation entirely, but I will always do my best to try and understand the situation as best I can."

'I thought that was such a weird thing, the fact that she can't experience what I might go through and will never fully understand it or feel it in the same way. Then my dad would tell me about the racism he experienced; he said that I likely wouldn't experience it to the same extent that he did. So, I felt a bit on my own with it. If neither of them can really understand the way the world sees me, how am I going to figure it all out on my own?'

Luke's experience reiterates to me that mixed people will never be able to 'pick a side'. It seems bizarre that society would pile on the pressure for mixed people to choose a side while simultaneously reinforcing that any decision they make is wrong. It was through being told, unequivocally, what he was not, that Luke was driven to find his identity in being mixed. How about, instead of society obsessing over whether we are more of one thing or another, we instead develop a better understanding and acceptance of what it means to sit between the two; to belong to both or neither categories?

Finding and defining identity as a mixed person is often about carving out a space for yourself where one didn't exist before. As previously mentioned, when I was born in 1988, there wasn't even an official way to record my identity adequately. So, it's no surprise that so many mixed people feel a longing to connect with each other, to push back against the singular labels that they don't always feel reflect who they are.

'Do I share the same identity as someone who is half Italian and half Moroccan just because I'm English and Jamaican?' Luke wondered. He was half asking himself, half asking me. He peppered every answer he gave me with these difficult questions – he seemed unafraid to interrogate his own feelings, consciously contradict himself, change his mind. It felt refreshing in a world where people usually feel the need to form solid, unmalleable opinions about everything.

'It can feel like we're being forced into something together. Are we forcing a collective identity for mixed people? Or should we just accept that everyone's different?'

Luke raises a valid point, and one that is often overlooked in conversations about mixed identity. The mixed population, in this country and around the world, is wildly heterogenous and cannot (and should not) be lumped together. Gender, space, class and wider structural issues can't be removed from conversations about identity. Racial identity never exists in a vacuum.

A person with mixed heritage who grew up during a different time in history, in a different part of the country, is likely to have a completely different set of lived experiences and therefore view their own identity from an entirely different perspective.

Joseph was born in the 1960s and grew up in Hull, East Yorkshire. Now he works as a journalist and editor in London, but his upbringing and experiences as a child in a predominantly white city more than half a century ago have shaped how he sees himself and how he chooses to identify.

'When I was growing up, you were just "half caste"', Joseph said. 'There was no positive at all about being mixed. You were this kind of mongrel child, loved by neither one nor the other.

'Hull was a very, very white city. I was the only brown face in school. I never knew my father – my Nigerian father – he left my mum before I was born. So I was the only element of difference in a 100 per cent white environment.'

I spoke to Joseph on Zoom because we were well into lockdown at that point. He must be a similar age to my dad. As we spoke, it struck me how infrequently I see people of mixed heritage who are my parent's generation. The gulf in our experiences of mixedness spans decades, and so much of what Joseph told me was new and unfamiliar to my own interpretation of identity. For one thing, the abuse and overt racism he faced growing up was so much worse than anything I have encountered first-hand.

'Mixed was not even talked about as a thing when I was growing up because there were so few of us. There was white, and there was me. I was treated as a complete outsider by white people. I got all the same sort of racial abuse as any Black kid would have got at that time. No one ever called me a "half nigger".'

Joseph has a similar skin tone to my own, and kind eyes. He manages to convey the kind of in-person warmth you rarely find on Zoom calls. To look at him it's quite clear to me that Joseph has some white heritage, but the fact that his skin was a shade or two lighter made absolutely no difference to the racists in his hometown when he was a kid.

'It was the 1960s. And now, we are not in any racial paradise by any means at all, but it is a healthy thing to remind ourselves of what it used to be like. People would just shout "nigger" at me across the street. Kids at school would do the same. At secondary school I had a teacher call me a "wog", and another teacher used the word "sambo" in class.

'My coping mechanism, not that I would have used that terminology back then, was to kind of laugh it off. Because if you don't laugh, you'll cry. The teacher who called me a "wog" was laughing when he said it; he thought it was a big joke to call me that. My mum came into school and complained, and he later apologised to me, but the teacher who used the word "sambo", I never got an apology for that.'

Later, at university, Joseph had bricks painted with Nazi swastikas thrown through his window. He says these experiences informed his opinions on mixedness, but also told him so much about white people's attitudes towards race.

'I experienced just how abusive children can be at a really young age – I'm talking six and seven years old. And remembering the way I was treated, the idea that I could ever cling on and pretend to be white – or that if I embraced my white side, I would be able to fit in – that was just very clearly never an option.

'We know that the darker skinned you are, the more discriminated against you're likely to be. The more African or foreign you sound, the more the more discriminated against you're likely to be. But certainly, being half white doesn't give you that many privileges. I have not found that. It certainly gives you privileges compared to darker-skinned Black people, but not in terms of whiteness.'

Joseph says he feels the same pressures as any Black man would when moving through the world. At work, in his majority white office, he feels pressure to be an ambassador, to be calm, serene, and non-threatening at all times. Whereas he feels 'posh white colleagues' could scream and get angry and shout as much as they like, he says he could never do that because he would be perceived as an angry, untrainable Black man.

'This love of mixedness that we have seen growing over the last maybe twenty years, it feels to me as though we are being used by white people to give the impression that they are not racist. We are celebrated and called "beautiful" because we are the acceptable face of Blackness. We're a bit white, so we're OK, we're a bit like them.'

But when Joseph was growing up, mixedness was denigrated, not celebrated. Mixed children were frequently presented as the products of unloving relationships, born out of wedlock, unwanted, something shameful.

'The children's homes were full of mixed-race kids because they were just given away because they were not wanted; because it was seen as a sort of embarrassment. Thankfully, my mum didn't see it like this, but at the time, mixed kids were very much seen as the cast-offs, the sad, lonely children who don't have a proper home. We were told – you're not Black, you're not white, you're this abnormal person in the middle.

'To see things turn around so much in my lifetime, when people would have been very happy to cast us out in those days, and now to be celebrating us as somehow these cool, great, young things . . . I think we have to be very wary of it.'

Joseph identifies as Black. He has never thought of himself as mixed. He also takes issue with the term 'mixed race'; like me, he doesn't like the implication that we are some kind of hybrid of two more pure states.

'I think the term is just as problematic as "half caste" because I think it implies that other people are pure and somehow, we are not,' he added.

'It also implies that we have a sort of a history in a culture, which we don't actually. Our culture is either Black or it's white, but there's not a mixed culture. And there's not a history. So, this concept of being "mixed race" sort of takes our roots away. We may have roots in white history or Black history, and it's up to us to decide which one we choose to identify with.

'I'm very proud to be Nigerian, and I'm very proud of my Irish background as well. My mum came over in the 1950s from Ireland, so those "no Blacks, no Irish, no dogs" signs were just as relevant to her as they would have been to my father at the time. I call myself Black and I don't consider that a rejection of my white half, that is just how I choose to be.'

Joseph believes that a single, collective identity for mixed people can't exist, and this may be true. But so many of my conversations with mixed Brits indicate that there are also recurring themes and experiences that tie the mixed experience together – in some ways, at least. It may not be possible to have a collective history, as Joseph points out, but there may be a sense of collective understanding in how we experience day-to-day life. And, if nothing else, some mixed people certainly long for this connection and union of identity.

There may be a generational element at play here. Joseph is in his fifties; he grew up at a time when mixedness was barely conceptualised in the UK, whereas people my age and younger may be more likely to find a sense of identity with others who also have mixed heritage, purely because we are more likely to know other mixed people, and because we now at least have officially recognised categories on the census. But the simple fact that there are more of us now doesn't mean that issues of identity are automatically easier for younger members of the mixed population.

Hannah is twenty-five and grew up in South London. Her mother is white Scottish and her father is from the Sudan, with Turkish and Egyptian heritage, but she has spent most of her life seamlessly navigating white spaces. Up until very recently, she hadn't given her identity, in terms of race, much thought at all, but looking back, she thinks being mixed has played a bigger part in who she is than she first gave it credit for.

'I forget that I'm brown,' Hannah explained. She was sitting across from me in the sunny atrium of my office building. Hannah has dark, straight hair, bright eyes and that rare ability to maintain a constant smile as she talks. She's definitely brown. She laughed easily. She reminded me of a lot of my own friends – that easy warmth and self-deprecating sarcasm.

'In the past when it's come up – my mixed-raceness – I've felt awkward about it. I'm so unaware of it generally that if someone says something that's in reference to the colour of my skin, I become coy about it because I kind of forgot. It's this otherness that you feel suddenly. A reminder that says, "By the way, you're different."'

All the way through her schooling, Hannah had white peer groups. She went to university in Glasgow where there was very little diversity, and hardly any other mixed people. It was all too easy for Hannah to forget that there was any difference between her and her white friends.

'Because you don't see yourself, you see the people around you, I saw almost exclusively white people. I always thought I was just the same as the people around me,' she said. We had met for a quick mid-morning coffee, but it quickly morphed into something like a therapy session. It seemed that it was cathartic for Hannah to talk about this stuff, she hadn't dug this deep into herself before – you could see it in the way the words poured out of her, the urgency of it.

'In Scotland, my experience was that if you look one way, you're Chinese. If you look another way, you're Indian. If you look another way, you're Black. And everyone else is just white. So, I was just "Indian" to everyone.'

Hannah knows she isn't white. At the basest level of understanding, of course she does. And there have been many moments throughout her life when she has been acutely aware of the fact that she is different. But she has often found herself lulled into a false sense of equality, and when she is reminded of this difference – always out of the blue – she is taken aback by the emotion that it throws up for her.

'I would be in this state of comfort, surrounded by my friends, and then someone would say something awkward or problematic about my race, and it always causes this weird, intense jolt,' said Hannah. She grimaced slightly at the memory – it was close to the surface.

'I always cry, or I feel myself welling up when it happens.

'Maybe it comes from feeling that you're completely alone. It is this instant isolation and it goes from suddenly being you, surrounded by your friends, to you, against everyone else. And there is no one there to back you up or even empathise. Suddenly it's just you, and you feel small.'

She suspected that it came down to the undermining of her identity, a questioning of who she is that she can never expect or understand, particularly from those closest to her. When forced to confront this question, it made her realise that she hadn't fully worked out the answer yet. I felt like I was watching her start to figure it out in real time.

'It is something that, for me, is so unexplored because I spend the majority of my time feeling exactly the same as my friends,' said Hannah. 'So, when they touch on my element of difference, it's my vulnerable spot.

'There is this glaringly obvious, physical indicator that I am not like everyone else. So, despite not always feeling that connection, reading stories about other mixed people has started that ball rolling for me. In my twenty-five years of life, I have never had these conversations with *anyone*. I can count on one hand the number of mixed people I know. Hearing about other people who just get it, I suddenly had this sense of recognition like – wait, I fit into that space.'

Recognition. Is it that? Is that the missing link that's needed in order to legitimise a sense of identity? Instead of a constant questioning and disbelief, maybe what we long for is the ability to see our experience of life reflected in the world around us and the people we talk to. I can understand that feeling, and Hannah certainly craved it.

'I think being mixed is the loneliest group. Mixed people, we can come together, but we're still singing from very different hymn sheets. That is the closest we ever feel to having a familiar, collective community, and even that is not *that* close to how I feel about my identity.'

She rolled her eyes and grinned broadly. She had a blasé, offhand manner when talking about something painful – it's a tactic I like to use too. But she was talking about isolation, and the smiles and shrugs didn't quite mask the sadness in her anecdotes. Hannah said that for most of her life, the very idea of race was only really spoken about in a negative context. It was the thing that made her different, the thing that made her life harder.

'It was the part of my identity that made me "other". It has been the reason people have said derogatory things to me. It's why I felt ugly growing up. It's why I've been called a Paki.'

When Hannah was younger, she used to wish she were white; she thought her life would be 'so much easier' if she looked like everyone else. It's not something she wants any more, but accepting her difference wasn't an easy process. She was at the very beginning of getting to grips with her identity; retrospectively piecing the elements together to figure out how ethnicity had affected her life and her place in the world and continued to do so. But she was still working out her motives – why should it matter to her? Why should she care?

'It feels crazy to me that I go about my everyday life looking a certain way and everyone seeing that but personally not connecting with it. That's mad. But at times it doesn't feel like much more than an obligation. Like this sense that I *should* learn about "where I come from", but I don't always know *why* I should. I have had lots of different influences in my life: people, events, places - none of them are connected to my mixed-raceness. That's fine. I'm very content with who I'm becoming; I don't feel like there is a big gap that needs to be filled.'

Before our conversation, Hannah told me she hadn't thought about this side of herself at all, but the fact that she chose to do this interview suggests a readiness – or even a need – to engage with her racial identity on a deeper level. She wanted to get to a point where her instant reaction to someone talking about her skin colour wasn't to burst into tears, and that was more important to her than any simplistic sense of obligation.

'It's so much easier to not engage with it. I think there's a part of me that begrudges the fact that I have to do this. That I have to grapple with all this complexity and find my place within it, when my white friends don't have to. That might be part of the reason why I pushed it away and ignored it for so long. Why do I have to consciously explore something about myself when they don't? But that's just white privilege, I guess. Not having to expend your energy to go through this process is a privilege that comes with being the majority group in a country.'

Hannah was working towards finding the words to be able to articulate – even just to herself – what being mixed means to her. And, clearly, that is something that is really important for her own conceptualisation of where she belongs in the world.

Identity politics has become an integral part of the social narrative in recent years. But the very phrase has been so overused that it has warped into something inherently negative. So now, any attempt to discuss identity in the public sphere can be shut down with a barrage of eye-rolling and accusations of irrelevance. But the eye-rollers and the critics are so often the people who fit perfectly inside one of society's pre-existing and accepted categories of identity. It's easy to bat these discussions away if the system works in your favour. But for those who don't fit, questions of identity are inescapably important, if not for you, then definitely for the people you come into contact with. Being questioned about your heritage, appearance, accent and legitimacy is a regular and exhausting reality for Black, brown and aesthetically non-white people in this country.

Hannah's story is a clear defence of identity politics – of the need to work out your place in the world in relation to others. The push towards 'post-racial' narratives is making it ever cooler to assert that who you are 'transcends race', that race simply 'doesn't matter'. But it's not true. Of course it matters – it can be the difference between feeling alone in the face of adversity and feeling as though you have back-up. Both Hannah and I can attest to the fact that attempting to simply ignore your racial identity can throw up some seriously disquieting emotions. It isn't progressive to look beyond colour; failing to acknowledge our differences can entrench divisions and leave us all feeling more disparate than ever.

For me, identifying as Black and mixed helps me make sense of my duality, the 'bothness' that makes me whole. It is comforting and empowering to know that there is a growing group that sits alongside me in this identity sphere. Within the UK mixed population, I think it's more than possible to acknowledge the elements that separate our experiences – gender, location, class, age and so on – while simultaneously recognising the many things that bind us; those universal experiences that act as a marker of collectivism. Hannah described the mixed population as the 'loneliest group', but that's not how I feel about it. We are in this together, and loudly claiming both our individual and collective identities is an antidote to isolation.

## *Half-stereotype* by Luke AG

*When I was younger I just wanted to be normal*
*And that was my biggest priority*
*But we were poorer than normal*
*And of course, I was a minority*
*So, becoming normal for me meant just being part of the majority*
*But everyone else's parents were normal*
    *and mine did choreography*

*That's wicked, I know, but where I grew up it was harder*
*All the other kids spent weekends with their parents and I was*
    *usually missing a father*

*They tried to make me do ballet or tap, but if I wanted to fit in*
    *I should rather*
*Play football in the park, or*
*Listen to Linkin Park, or*
*Pretend the other kids on the playground didn't call me half-*
    *caste, or*

*Hide in plain sight*
*And keep my Afro cut low*
*Speak the Queen's English*
*Like everybody I know*

*I used to win every race on the athletics track*
*Until I learned to run slow*

*Because every time I won, they said*
*The only reason I did is because I'm Black*
*And ignored the fact that I spent 10,000 hours training on that*
    *track*

*They called me Black until I tried to rap,*

*Then they told me I wasn't Black enough*
*'Because you speak white and your skin's light and you*
  *'Study too much'*

*Eventually I gave up trying to be 'normal'*
*Because I realised to them, being 'normal'*
*Meant being white*
*But deep down, I knew that wasn't right*
*But I never had any Black people to tell me that in my life, so I*

*Constructed my identity as half white and half stereotype.*

*Feeling excluded from white society as the perpetual other*
*Then looking into the eyes of another Black person*
*And not understanding one another*
*Looking into the eyes of your own mother*
*And realising that*
*You're not the same ethnicity as one another*

*It's like Afua Hirsch says, it's hard being British*
*Especially when you're Brit-ish*
*Three generations deep and they're still asking where I'm from . . .*
*And I usually say Britain, but maybe I'm wrong*

*Because I'm a little bit Scottish*
*And a little bit Greek*
*My grandparents came from Jamaica*
*But my grandad looks like a Sikh*
*He came from Cuba*
*So it must've been kind of peak*
*But at the end of the day*
*I don't really know where they came from.*

*Puts my petty identity crises in some light*
*But there's something about being mixed race in Britain*

*That makes you feel like you're not right*
*Understanding your identity*
*Only comes once you understand your own mind*
*And I don't understand mine*
*That doesn't mean I'm not trying*
*Maybe one day I will*
*But until then, I've got to leave this poem*
*Half-fin . . .*

# Chapter 2

# Family

It's July and it's warm enough for bare legs. It's my granddad's 80th birthday party and it is quite the event. Brian, my mum's dad, loves a party. He is never the type to shy away from the spotlight and turns up to everything with bells on, half an hour earlier than everyone else, and if the kettle isn't on when he steps through the door there'll be trouble. This is a man who sounds just as cockney now as when he left Twickenham for the bright lights of the Midlands more than half a century ago. He rings the bells at his village church, jets off on holiday every chance he gets, and he was delivering meals-on-wheels to the old folk in his village long after he was old enough to qualify for them himself. 'A moving target is harder to hit,' says Brian of old age. Or death. He loves my little sister and I fiercely, and boasts about us to everyone he knows, every chance he gets. He is the only granddad we have ever known or needed.

We grew up in white spaces. The suburb in Cheshire, South Manchester, where we lived was mostly white, our schools were mostly white, and, due to a variety of circumstances – namely distance and old resentments – it was my mum's side of the family, my white family, who have always had a much bigger influence on my life (although the balance is now starting to even out ever so slightly). My place within this family is certainly a defining part of my own identity; the lessons they have taught me, the values they have instilled in me, the ridiculous things I find funny because of them.

Our Christmases, weddings and birthdays are frenetic, hilarious events fuelled by red wine, good food, endless in-jokes and a lot of love. I belong to them in the truest sense of the word, so much so that it's incredibly easy to forget that there is a fundamental element of difference there; that my sister and I are a different ethnicity. In fact, it never comes up. It's so rare that anything ever draws my attention to this difference, but I guess that makes it even more destabilising when it does happen.

It's that warm, July day, the day of the party, and we are standing in the village hall where the dark wooden furnishings and exposed beams have been spruced up with tablecloths and fairy lights. Guests shimmer briefly as they cut across the chunk of sunlight that dissects the hall where the fire escape has been thrown open into a dazzling afternoon. There's a small stage at the far end where a band is tuning up, preparing to revive the sounds of the 1950s – granddad's glory years. A full pig with its head still attached roasts in an endless pirouette under a gazebo just outside the entrance. This is middle England, quite literally: Stowe-by-Chartley, a tiny village almost in the dead-centre of England, just outside of Stafford, small enough to sprint from one end to the other. My sister Becky and I are the only non-white faces in the room. And we are comfortable with that. It's how we spent large portions of our childhood; we barely notice it.

Mum is outside, unloading tray after tray of potato salad from our tiny car. The hour's drive from Manchester that morning was a teetering balancing act, everyone holding a tray, pinning the cling film down at the edges with clammy fingers, more trays stuffed between our feet, precariously wedged under the back window. The car filling with the smell of sweet mayonnaise and onions as the mid-morning sun began to bake us through the windows. In the boot were more trays which held Mum's vegetarian stuffing which, we found out later, had the consistency of almost-set concrete. We still don't talk about the stuffing.

I'm wearing a charity shop find – a dusky pink tea dress with a high neck and a hem that falls just below my knee. It has a frothy underskirt and a giant bow at the back that sits at the base of my spine. I've teamed it with nude, strappy block heels that, miraculously, don't hurt my feet. My curls are swept up on top of my head, pinned in a sleek bun. It's too warm for a jacket. My boyfriend Jared is wearing light chinos and a fitted white shirt. I'm showing him off. Granddad keeps calling him 'heartthrob' and pulling him close for chats. I am delighted at their conspiratorial bonding.

The band starts up and Granddad dances with every woman in the room. His energy is infectious, and he becomes a fizzing source of light at the centre of the hall. We devour the pig, and everyone eats the potato salad. No one eats the stuffing. The sun sets but the lingering warmth of the day pours itself through the open windows and we keep dancing. Granddad takes my hand and spins me wildly before hugging me in and telling me for the eighteenth time that evening how proud he is of me. My mum and aunty are drinking gin and laughing a touch too loudly at a table in the corner. I find my sister and link my arm through hers.

Everyone in the village is here. The old women are enamoured with my sister and I, and we tower over them, almost six foot a piece – and that's without our heels on. They call us 'Amazonian', 'modelesque', 'exotic'; they don't see many women who look like us in real life. Becky and I smile and smile. We are used to this; we don't mind the attention.

We find Jared and embark on a mission to find a fresh bottle of white wine, but our progress to the makeshift bar in the kitchen is impeded by an older lady whom none of us recognise. She wants to chat.

'Oh my goodness, absolutely stunning, just stunning, aren't they,' the woman says, half to us and half to her husband who is standing, mute, alongside her, his face impassive.

'How tall are you?' she asks Becky and I, collectively. She is well into her eighties. Her skin is impossibly wrinkled; deep yet fragile creases transform her face into an off-white sheet of discarded crepe paper. There is a tiny smudge of dark lipstick on her front tooth.

'We're cheating, don't worry,' I say, pointing at my heels with a smile. The bland, self-deprecating line I trot out whenever anyone remarks on our height. She enjoys this. We smile and smile.

'So, how do you know Brian?' she asks Jared. I flick a quick glance at Becky, she's staring hard at this tiny woman. Any emotion that Becky feels is instantly apparent on her face; her eyes are less a window to her soul, more a barn door thrown open for everyone to see inside. Right now, she's wary, but still happy to play nice.

'Oh, well, Nat's my girlfriend,' says Jared, resting a hand on my shoulder. The woman looks at me blankly and then back at Jared.

'Right?' The lines between her eyebrows furrow to a cavernous depth.

'And . . . Nat is Brian's granddaughter. And Becky is too,' Jared nods his head towards my sister. Everyone stares at everyone.

A visible wave of pure confusion seems to sweep through the woman's entire body, before her eyes change and she lets out a bark of a laugh that stings the air like a slap. She laughs at us again, hard, and shakes her head at Jared. She thinks it's a joke. The band strikes up a new number and everyone behind us cheers.

When we don't laugh with her, the woman yanks her husband's hand and leads him away towards the stage, still laughing to herself and shaking her head as though we had pulled the prank of the century. We all stand for a moment, frozen as the aftershocks ripple through us. Becky's face folds into a caricature of outraged astonishment, but only for an instant. We shake it off and return to our hunt for wine.

This isn't what I remember when I think about this party. It's there, of course, but it was such an impossibly fleeting moment that it in no way eclipses the whirling, happy memories of that night. The overwhelming sense of contentment, the laughter that hurt my face, the moment my sister fell in a bush on our wobbly, wine-addled walk back to Granddad's house. But this tiny interaction does show up the discordance that can be triggered by being visibly different in terms of race to the rest of your relatives, and the importance that other people place on aesthetics and phenotypical traits when considering notions of family.

It would be easy to chalk this awkward moment up to individual ignorance. This woman was of a different generation, living in a rural village in middle England, and while this isn't really an excuse, it might be an explanation. Given her life experience, it's likely she would have little to no understanding of the concept of interracial families. But really, the lack of understanding, and inherent suspicion of interracial marriages and resulting children, is still widespread, and not necessarily confined to the elderly or those who have lived sheltered lives. It often comes from a darker, more intentionally hostile place.

Some people still hold the belief that interracial families are deviant and doomed to fail; that there is something intrinsically wrong or 'unnatural' about 'racial mixing'. It's an archaic prejudice that stems from faulty interpretations about what race actually is, and in some cases, it is linked to vague and dangerous notions about 'racial purity'. This stick-to-your-own mentality has influenced human behaviour for centuries and it still pervades today.[1] The old lady didn't say any of this of course, but it's probable she was, maybe unconsciously, thinking along these lines. The idea that Becky and I could be related to Brian was so unthinkable for her that all she could do was laugh in our faces.

In September 2019, Lidl used a real-life, interracial family as part of an advertising campaign. Fiona Ryan, who is white Irish and her partner Jonathan Mathis, who is Brazilian but grew up in Liverpool, featured in the billboard campaign with their 22-month-old son Jonah. Soon after the billboards went up, the couple started receiving racist abuse online, including death threats to both them and their toddler son. It got so bad they even made the decision to leave their home in County Meath, Ireland, and move to England. It is unbelievable to me that in 2019, a family is being forced to flee their home, flee the entire country, because people threatened to kill them and their child for no reason other than their interracial union. It's terrifying.

---

1 Stephanie B. Guy, Yvonne Ayo, Roger Bullock, Dinah Morley, 'Breaking Stereotypes with Data: A Report on Mixed Race Children and Families in the UK', People in Harmony Research Report, 28th January, 2018

'I was so shaken I broke down in tears,' Fiona told the *Irish Post*[2]. 'It was the last straw and, yes, we decided we really need to lay low, to leave. We booked flights. We just thought, "Could they actually find us if we stay where we are?" If my 22-month-old son has to live in a country that doesn't protect his right to be who he is, then I'm not going to live in a country that does that to my child.'

Some tweets accused Lidl of the 'replacement' of white people, others accused the couple of 'race/ancestor betrayal', words that smack of brazen white supremacy and a deep-seated fear of difference. At the heart of the torrents of abuse were tweets by an Irish former journalist and a host of nasty, fired-up followers, and this reaction was extreme and incredibly unfortunate for the family involved – but it isn't an anomaly. We are increasingly seeing this kind of rhetoric, and it's scary. It doesn't take much to tip over from 'concern' about the longevity or success rate of an interracial family, to open hatred and hostility. They are two branches of the same tree.

My childhood was overwhelmingly happy and whole. Dad wasn't living with us for most of it, but he was there for us, all of us, in a way that I rarely saw from friends' parents who were still together. I'm writing this with an awareness that I was seven at the time they broke up, a natural daddy's girl and that I was more than likely shielded from any real unpleasantness or drama that may have occurred when my parents split. But what I saw was Dad coming over for family dinners three times a week, driving me to endless netball sessions and Becky to singing classes, spending every weekend whisking us all over for swimming, theme parks, cinema trips and tromping through every single country park in the north-west of England. I saw

2   Rachel O'Connor, Irish Post, 27th September 2019

my parents trying really hard – they even got back together for a year when I was eleven (this ended up being confirmation that it was *definitely* not going to work). Dad wasn't there for a lot of the tough stuff, the day-to-day stuff, the screaming matches as my sister morphed into a perpetually pissed-off teenager, but our little nucleus of family was strong and whole, if not always in the traditional sense. We weren't broken, we were perfectly imperfect, anchored by love.

I know my own family history, how it has shaped me as a person and informed my beliefs, but my singular story isn't enough to debunk the negative and pervasive stereotype that an interracial relationship will automatically translate to a broken home. I was interested to find out if others shared my view, if there were more families with their own unique, nuanced and perfectly imperfect stories to tell. I had to take a wider look at mixed family life, beyond my own experiences, to chip away at these old misconceptions and get closer to the reality.

One of the people I spoke to on the subject was Ciaran, a youth worker and writer with a focus on social justice, youth violence and London's rap scene, specifically drill music. Ciaran's dad is Indian, Punjabi, and his mum is white British; mainly English and a bit Irish. Like me, his interracial family has been a source of strength and a tool to build resilience and adaptability. Ciaran says he spends his life moving back and forth between two camps, but he doesn't feel torn or stretched by this; on the contrary, he tells me it's enriching.

'If my parents did it deliberately, then well done to them. They didn't often talk explicitly about race, but they certainly gave my sisters and I a lot of opportunities to explore it ourselves: through things like the schools we were sent to, upholding traditions in the family home, and travel.'

37

Ciaran has only been to India three times, but each visit was comprehensive. He says there is a feeling he gets when he lands in Delhi, or any north Indian city – especially in the Punjab – that just feels like home. An instant belonging. And he says his Indian family in the UK has helped him form this attachment.

'It sounds corny, I know. I think a lot of it is to do with the smells, the language, the noise and the street food; all of which I will have been experiencing and learning about since day one; from going to Southall to visit my family.'

Southall is commonly nicknamed 'little India'. More than 55 per cent of Southall's population is Indian or Pakistani; some sources say that the West London borough has the largest Punjabi community outside India, and over the years it has been a vitally important hub for millions of South Asians who have come to Britain.

'When I go to Southall, I get this crazy nostalgia. You're not going to find anywhere else on the planet that is more of a hybrid between India and England. I had a really loving, warm grandparental home there that allowed me to feel that sense of belonging.'

Ciaran's experience with his family pushes back against the destabilisation argument; the idea that interracial families cause inherent turmoil for mixed children. Ciaran has found the opposite. Even when his cousins in India made jokes at his expense, referring to him as 'gora', which means 'white boy', he says it didn't feel at all malicious.

'They were actually almost showing me off, and I find it funny. Even regardless of being mixed race, my mannerisms and the way I talk and dress are going to be like a Western person to them, so I get why they say that and why they see me like that.

'I've only ever experienced the feeling of exclusion on grounds of race from white people. I've never experienced it from other British Asians, like my friends at school. I only ever felt welcomed by and treated as one of them. The same is true of my Asian family: they always made my sisters and I feel included, even if it was still acknowledged that we were the half-white kids out of all the cousins.'

This reminds me of the instant warmth I felt when I first started to make connections with Dad's wider family, my Black cousins, aunties and uncles who are dotted around Manchester, London, Washington and all over Jamaica. There was an immediate welcoming of all of us, a clear desire to draw us into their unit. They pulled us in and claimed us as their own without question.

After almost a lifetime of estrangement, and a deep reluctance to even talk about his family, Dad began to rebuild those bridges in the last few years of his life. He started speaking to his biological mother, Pauline, with regular phone calls to Jamaica, and when his father, Carl, got sick, Dad went to see him and made his peace with him before he slipped away. For my sister and I, this opened the door to the rest of our family – the cousins and second cousins, aunties and uncles, all so funny and loving and full of life. Our support system doubled overnight, and we were embraced completely into the fold.

Unlike Ciaran, one thing I never had to contend with when forging these connections was a language barrier. He admits he found himself locked out of certain conversations and still feels regret at not having learnt the language when he was a child. There were times when he felt like he was missing out, and even though it was never malicious, no amount of welcome or warmth could help to bridge that distance.

'Everyone would burst out into hysterics and I would ask – what's funny? Only to be told it isn't funny if you translate it into English. That was frustrating, it remains frustrating.' Ciaran told me that he intends to learn Punjabi as a way of understanding himself and unlocking his family history more completely.

'Even though I was sometimes excluded by language, it wasn't a deliberate thing; it would just make sense to tell those stories in Punjabi for my granddad or my grandma, aunties and uncles. Even if it was disappointing on one level, I never held that against anyone. I genuinely feel like my immediate family did such a great job of embracing both sides of my heritage.'

On the face of it, Ciaran's experience sounds like the picture-perfect blending of two worlds, but it's never as straightforward as that. People have a tendency to oversimplify what it means to be part of a mixed family and attach huge cultural or social significance to our very existence, as though we're not just normal families with ups and downs, good and bad moments, like everyone else.

Alongside the hostility and suspicious scrutiny that inter-racial families face from the wider public, sits a specific kind of romanticisation that stems directly from this kind of over-simplification. One reading of Ciaran's account of his family dynamic seems to play into this romantic notion; the idea that interracial families act as some kind of symbolic, cultural bridge – an emblem of progress, the idea that mixed families hold the key to a luminous future without racism.

'If we can't slot people into familiar categories, perhaps we'll be forced to reconsider existing definitions of race and identity, presumptions about who is us and who is them,' suggests Lise

Funderburg[3], author of *Black, White, Other: Biracial Americans Talk About Race and Identity*. 'Perhaps we'll all end up less parsimonious about who we feel connected to.'

Funderburg appears here to be nudging close to the popular notion that a growing mixed population will ultimately lead to racial harmony. People who subscribe to this idea are generally fond of using terms like 'golden generation' and 'colourblind', and they think that the very existence of mixed people points to a world where racism won't be a thing any more. How can people be racist or hold on to racial prejudice if they're willing to start a family with someone of a different ethnic background? And when everyone is eventually a light shade of golden brown, racism will finally be done, finished, finito. In some people's minds, it is really that simple.

It's a nice idea. Of course, we want to believe that something so straightforward could theoretically solve racism. This solution also conveniently places the onus of tackling this problem not on white society – who created and perpetuate racism – but on minorities and their children. By placing the responsibility of deconstructing centuries of systemic racism on the shoulders of a future, mixed generation to solve this problem simply by existing, those who uphold a belief in this 'golden generation' are failing to look back; to rigorously dissect the past and evaluate the systems in place that still actively oppress millions today.

But that sounds like hard work, right? And it requires an acceptance of responsibility, which people in power are historically not great at doing, hence the desire to lean towards this simplistic view of a 'post-racial' mixed future. It is much less

---

3   Lise Funderburg, 'The Changing Face of America', National Geographic, October 2013

work to believe that the hopes of societal harmony lie with a majority-mixed population of the future than to actually examine the systemic causes of inequality.

The implication of this argument is that the very existence of mixed people can somehow aid conflict resolution and cure society of its need to compete, dominate and divide. That a generation of thoroughly and equally mixed people will undermine racial hierarchies and fix everything that's wrong with the world. But I don't buy it. It reads like a superficial idolisation of mixed people (and even within that, only those of us who fit a specific aesthetic) and ignores the implications and causes of racism that run so much deeper than skin tone.

There's also clear evidence in the world already that it just doesn't work. You only have to look at Latin America to see that a majority-mixed population is not an automatic answer for removing, or even reducing, racism. In Latin America, 'racial mixing' has been going on for 500 years, and a majority of the people in those countries would describe themselves as mixed. And yet, we still see clear racism in these societies. That is, in part, due to the fact that some people see themselves as more European and less indigenous than others – so even if we are all mixed in the future, people will find a way to create divisions and hierarchies. That's just what humans do. Also, the way 'race' has been constructed historically was never simply about skin colour, it was about creating systems for colonial powers to 'other' certain groups while maintaining their own power. Skin colour is often just a convenient short-hand for defining and separating these groups. Even if in the future everyone really did look similar, would this really be enough to undermine the systems of power that are at the heart of our racial constructions?

'The idea that a growing mixed-race population will offer some kind of cure for racism is highly idealistic and even dangerous,' Dr Remi Joseph-Salisbury, a sociology professor at Manchester University, explained to me.[4]

'Such ideas belie the deep-rooted nature of racism and run counter to the historical and contemporary lived experiences of mixed-race people. The desire to romanticise mixed-race people as a solution to society's racial ills is not reflective of reality. It is only reflective of the kind of stories that society would like to believe about itself.

'To bring an end to racism, society would really need to grapple with its past and to consider how its institutions systematically disadvantage racially minoritised communities. This is a far greater task than merely celebrating Meghan Markle.'

Remi is right to call it romanticising. The 'golden generation' theory is an easy out. It's a way for people to avoid doing the serious, complicated, difficult work of examining their own history, examining their part to play in perpetuating racism, examining how deep-rooted inequalities are still very much part of our society *today*, not in some abstract, utopian future.

The growth of the mixed population should never be used as a shield against accusations of racism because the two things can absolutely exist alongside each other, but it frequently is. We know that racism can exist within mixed families, that white people with mixed children can be racist, that mixed people can perpetuate anti-Blackness and colourism, and this is why the simple presence of mixed families can never be a quick fix in dismantling racial hierarchies. It will take so much more than simple symbolism.

---

4   Natalie Morris, 'Racism "won't go away" even if we're all mixed-race in the future', Metro.co.uk, 18th June, 2019

Dating, sleeping with, marrying or even having children with a person of a different ethnicity, doesn't mean you can't be racist. Mixed people can experience overt racial hostility from members of their own family[5]. And yet it is so often used as a defence: 'I can't be racist; my wife is Black.' 'I can't be racist; I have mixed kids.' But that's not how it works.

Ciaran knows this. Racist attitudes from two generations before his parents led to divisions and hostility from certain sections of the family, the full details of which are only just starting to emerge for him. And, in keeping with the research that says white people are more likely to be disapproving of interracial relationships, it was older members of the white side of Ciaran's family that presented any problems, with some struggling to accept his parents' marriage.

'My late gramps - may he rest in peace - was a complex character. He ultimately never expressed any problem about my parents' decision to marry and was always very supportive. Still, he used the words "darkie" and "wog" in front of me. Hearing them come from his mouth, whether he was talking about Black people or Asian people, even if I knew that he meant no harm, and that his way was just a product of an outdated, less tolerant time, made me feel physically sick. I remember being a teenager, sitting at the dinner table at my grandparents' home in Farnborough, Hampshire, unable to swallow my food or express how angry I was. And his dad, my great-granddad, well, that's a whole story in itself.'

Ciaran's great-granddad had a really close relationship with Ciaran's mum for the majority of her life. At the age of 19, when she decided she was going to marry Ciaran's dad, she went

5  K L Nadal et al, 'Microaggressions Within Families: Experiences of Multiracial People', Family Relations, Vol. 62, Issue 1, February 2013

to tell her granddad and invite him to the wedding, but to her complete bemusement, he kicked her out of the house and said he wouldn't be coming to the wedding under any circumstances. He had been OK with the relationship but, in his eyes, getting married overstepped the mark. It was all the more upsetting because it came out of nowhere; she had absolutely no idea that he would have a problem with her marrying an Indian man.

When her granddad – who was Irish but fought for the British in Burma in the Second World War – was lying on his deathbed, Ciaran's mum took Ciaran, as a baby, to meet his great-granddad for the first time. He had always expressed a deep wish for a grandson and Ciaran's mum thought this meeting would help to reconcile the differences, but he refused to see the baby and died without ever laying eyes on Ciaran. His wife, Ciaran's great-gran, remained in close contact with Ciaran's mum; Ciaran has many fond memories of spending time with her as a toddler before she passed away.

'My grandma only told me her perspective at the end of last year. She said that she had literally never told anyone some of its details before. When it was all going on, her and my gramps had spent a lot of time trying to persuade my great-grandad, her father-in-law, to go to my parents' wedding. But he never budged, and I know he said some very hurtful things in the process. And these conversations had been locked in her head for years  before we spoke about them.

'She's an amazing woman. She has started going to pensioner history classes – I found it hilarious – she said she was learning about British history that she hadn't known about before, and she said, "We really were buggers, weren't we?"'

Ciaran attributes some problematic attitudes held by people in older generations to gaps in education. He says that if people his age were not taught about the true impacts and implications of British colonialism at school, what hope did people who were brought up in the 1940s and '50s have of getting a realistic picture of Britain's role in global history?

'My girlfriend Yasmin – who is also mixed, French and Pakistani – and I have way more of a language to talk about racism than our Asian parents did when they were our age, even though they would have experienced a lot more racism than we ever have. I would never want to take away agency from those generations, but I think it's a lot to do with the need for assimilation. I feel like they felt pressure to accept what came their way and play down their "otherness" at any cost.'

This desire to avoid these kinds of conversations that Ciaran describes makes me think of my dad, too; his reluctance to talk about his family, about the intergenerational pain caused by the displacement of immigration, about the abuse and hostility I know he must have faced as a Black child growing up with a white foster mother in a white coastal town in the 1970s. And yet, he so rarely spoke about it. He was more likely to attribute his own struggles in life to class and an institutionalised upbringing than anything to do with race.

There are so many parallels to draw between Ciaran's experience with his family and my own, but what is clear for both of us is that our interracial families are neither glowing bastions of hope nor inherently doomed and deviant. So, what are we? Well, we don't have to *be* anything. The argument here is again to recognise our heterogony; to push back against simplistic, collective interpretations of mixed families that lump us all into one group. To imply that families like mine, Ciaran's and millions of others, can really have any singular, unifying significance caused simply by our mixedness – positive or negative – makes no sense at all.

The beauty of mixed families, like all families, is in our quirks, imperfections, anecdotes and in-jokes; the things that make us cry with laughter, infuriate us to the point of life-long feuds, the things that make us truly individual. We are so much more than an idealistic 'bridge' between two worlds, and so much less at the same time. It isn't flattering to be told that our families are the future of humanity; it's lazy, and it drags many of us into a narrative that we have no interest in and are not equipped to be part of. The brilliance of mixed families comes not from our aesthetic potential to head up 'progressive' advertising campaigns, or our 'magical' ability to heal humanity's cultural divides; it comes from our undeniable ordinariness.

You see this normality in the vastly varied ways we all operate as families, and in the fact that interracial families are not actually a new phenomenon, as is so often presumed (particularly in certain articles that love to herald the mixed-race population as the 'new' face of Britain).

'Interraciality in Britain has much older, wider, and diverse roots,' writes Chamion Caballero in a 2019 paper. She explains that mixed relationships, families and people in Britain are documented as early as the sixteenth century, and that a defining quality of their existence is how normal this was. Her eye-opening research finds interracial families existing at every cross-section of society, rural areas and the city, the working classes and the elite – they were and continue to be a phenomenon not restricted by class, location or time period.

She says that not only was the presence of interracial families in Britain commonplace, but their experiences of life were unremarkable as well. Her study includes first-hand accounts of the banalities and mundaneness of everyday mixed life in Britain from the late 1800s into the early and mid-1900s:

'accounts of "ordinariness" – of presence and experience – that disrupt the traditional pathological narratives'.

But, while their presence may have been more common-place than you might have assumed, mixed families in Britain over previous centuries faced much higher rates of racism, hostility and demonisation than they do today. White mothers were shamed, non-white parents were frequently viewed as inferior or dangerous and their mixed children were pitied and pathologised. In 1930, the *Daily Express* ran an article entitled 'The Street of Hopeless Children', which detailed the lives of the many mixed children who lived in Crown Street, a road in East London. The article calls these children 'poor little half-castes', and says their lives are 'barren of almost everything but dirt, disease and despair, without race, with no country that they can call their own'.

'Certainly, many of the mixed-race people, couples and families in early-twentieth century Britain faced extraordinary levels of racism directed towards them, not only that which condemned and stigmatised them socially, but that which manifested through policy and practice,' reads an extract from *Mixed Race Britain in the Twentieth Century*, a book by Caballero and Peter J. Aspinall.[6] On the flip side though, when looking at the personal recollections of British people who actually lived among these mixed families, as opposed to the official records and media reports read by the middle classes with no direct experience, Caballero and Aspinall found a more 'multi-layered and inclusive' attitude towards interracial relationships. They say interviews taken from diverse areas of London in the 1930s 'suggest a picture of a community

6   Chamion Caballero and Peter J. Aspinall, 'Mixed Race Britain in the Twentieth Century', Palgrave Macmillan, London, 2018

in which mixed families and people were not only visible but accepted'.

This tendency to view interracial families as either pathological and inherently doomed, or as humanity's glowing hope for the future, is often tied into a mistaken belief that mixed families are a *new* phenomenon and, as such, are a deviation from the norm. But, as Caballero's study clearly proves, mixed families are very much part of the normal fabric of British society and have been for centuries.

'Bringing narratives of ordinariness to the fore,' writes Caballero, 'is one means of disrupting dominant conceptualisations – either pathological or celebratory – and providing space for new understanding and perceptions of the presence and experiences of interraciality in Britain to emerge'.

Annalisa is one of those people who has a different experience of interraciality, particularly when it comes to her upbringing. Annalisa's biological mother is white, Welsh, and her biological father is Black, Jamaican. But she was adopted by two Black Jamaican parents.

'I identify as both Black and mixed race. I have always had it instilled in me by my family that I am Black, but I would feel that if I didn't acknowledge the mixed part of my identity, I would be in some ways denying the adopted side of me, and I would never want to do that,' she explains.

We're finally speaking over Skype after weeks of rearranged meetings; Annalisa had been struggling to finish her dissertation after spilling coffee on her laptop three days before the submission date and losing thousands of words – truly the stuff of nightmares. When we spoke, she was studying a post-grad in communications and when she wasn't wrestling with her essay deadlines, she was spending her time working to elevate the voices of the Black community in Sheffield, where she lives.

'Growing up, my mum and dad have always been invested in teaching me about my Black history; where I've come from, my heritage and what it means to be Black. There was an incident where my mum marched down to my school because they were teaching us about Florence Nightingale, and Mum was like, "No, you should be learning about Mary Seacole."'

Annalisa recognises that she hasn't necessarily had the most 'typical' upbringing as a mixed individual, if such a thing exists. She says that discussions she's had recently with other mixed people (and she's mainly talking about people with Black and white heritage) have made her realise that her experiences growing up have been different, and she says that comes from not having to navigate whiteness within her own family.

'A mixed-race person said to me, "You can't understand this because you've grown up with Black parents. If you had a white parent, you'd understand." Over the years I have also had some contentious conversations with mixed-race people, particularly when it comes to discussions about proximity to whiteness, for example.'

Annalisa says it can be difficult having discussions about white privilege with other mixed people because her family is entirely Black, which she says gives her a different perspective to mixed people who have white relatives. She has had clashes with friends and colleagues in the past over different opinions on these issues.

I think about my own family when Annalisa says this. The dominant whiteness of my upbringing, existing as a minority in village halls, surrounded by people who love me but can't experience the world as I do. It took me until my late twenties to settle on the self-identification of Black and mixed. Would Annalisa have clashed with me about the way I used to speak about my heritage, and my previous obliviousness to my own proximity to white privilege? There's definitely a part of me that envies Annalisa for knowing her place in the world so definitely and with such conviction.

'I started a festival in Sheffield for Black History Month, which was something that has never been done in Sheffield – it has always kind of been left off the council's radar,' she says. 'When we were building the festival there were a few different views within the team on how we were trying to navigate in it.

'I was very much like; it's *Black* History Month. This is for Black people, we centre Black people, whereas other people on the team were a bit like, "Well, no, because I want my white family to be able to come to this and I want white people to be able to come." But I stuck to my position. It's Black History Month so we centre Black people.'

Annalisa says attitudes towards multiculturalism in Sheffield verge on the utopian. She says people are always striving for unity and 'colour blindness', which she thinks can be a damaging rhetoric, but she sometimes finds it hard to get her views across.

'We need to appreciate our differences, and doing that does create cohesion,' she explains.

'We can't be colour blind. And I think sometimes those views do clash with the views of some other mixed-race people, particularly here in Sheffield, because it feels like people just want to create a family of one, which is great in theory, but we also need to realise that within that one, there are many differences that shouldn't be erased.'

Annalisa's family experience is atypical to that of most mixed people in that her parents – the people who brought her up – are of the same race. It occurs to me that this may, in part, account for the strength in Annalisa's conviction when it comes to ideas about mixedness, Blackness and her own self-identity. It was never in question because she was receiving a singular, consistent message at home. At the same time, she feels she can't discount the impact of her biological parents and how they may have contributed to who she is.

'My birth grandma, she was a racist and she didn't want a mixed-race child in her family. That's literally how I ended up being put up for adoption. I'd love to meet my birth mum because she did want to look after me. She was really upset. She didn't want to give me up for adoption.' Annalisa's biological mum struggled with mental illness and wasn't well enough to look after a child. And with no support from her mother, she felt that she didn't have any other option. So now, Annalisa has made the decision to search for her birth mother. She has questions for her and wants to know more about her, but the timing is tricky.

'My mum – the woman who raised me – has terminal cancer. She was diagnosed last August and she's lucky that she's still here. She was given a few months to live. She should have died last December, but she's still here.

'So, I probably wouldn't do it now. I wouldn't want to upset her. Even though she has always told me that if I wanted to find my birth mother, she would be fine with that, I know that my parents are quite sensitive when it comes to this. They have always been open with me about everything, but I know this is a touchy issue for them. My sister found her birth parents and, I think at the time, it hurt my mum quite a lot. So, I have always been cautious.'

But she says that when the time is right, she will do her best to find them. She wants to know more about her heritage, where she comes from, and to find out more about the lives of the couple who conceived her; how they came to be together in the face of clear racism on her mum's side at least.

'I'm thirty-three this year, and I don't know if my birth parents are dead or alive. When I was younger, I always thought I would find my parents when I was settled; when I had a career, when I had this, when I had that. As I'm getting older, I'm realising that I'm not going to get to the place that I hoped I would be at before I found them, so I've just got to do it.

'I want to know why I am the way I am, because in many ways, I'm so different to my adoptive parents. They are both so quiet, so serious, which is so not me. My adoption papers say that I had leadership qualities at the age of two, and I want to know where I get that fire from.'

Joseph's Nigerian father disappeared from his life before he was born. So, like Annalisa, he grew up with this nagging feeling of wanting to know more, like there was a hole in his personal history that needed to be filled. As Joseph told us in *Identity*, he grew up in the 1960s in Hull, and he was brought up by his Irish mother and his adopted father, who was also white.

'We only ever really spoke about race in the sense that, if I had been abused at school that day, then I might mention it. There was a period of time where there were lots of conversations because I was reacting to being abused.

'Typically, the white teachers would say I was the trouble-maker, and I was getting into trouble for reacting to what the other kids were saying and doing to me. The people who were doing the abusing never faced consequences at all.'

For Joseph, these conversations were tricky. How do you talk about these things as the only Black child in a white family? As the only non-white child in your entire school? How can anyone possibly understand what you're going through?

'It's an experience that they will never have,' said Joseph. 'My mum would have identified to some extent being Irish – being Irish in England during the 1950s and '60s was pretty rough as well – but it's not exactly the same thing.

'I was just told: don't react, then it will go away. And that sort of worked. But it still leaves you thinking, "I'm still different. I'm still inferior. Everyone is telling me I am worth less." Looking back now, I think some sense of my history and identity would have been good to have. It would have helped so much to have a sense of belonging to something. I never felt I belonged to anything.'

Joseph's first job was working for *The Voice* newspaper, a Black news publication based in London, and it was a transformative experience for him. It was the late 1980s, and after graduating from university, Joseph had finally found a space where he didn't stick out, where he wasn't constantly seen as 'other', somewhere where he belonged.

'There were Black people of all shades, all colours. We were kind of this rainbow coalition. Caribbeans and small islanders, Jamaicans and West Africans, and mixed-race people, and people just like me with a parent missing.'

It was within a year of starting at *The Voice* that Joseph left for Nigeria to try to find his father. He was only twenty-five and travelled alone, having no idea where his dad lived, what he might be doing, and with only a single grainy photo of his father taken in 1962 for reference.

'I did track him down,' he told me. 'I found out from his name which part of Nigeria he came from and actually managed to locate the village where he lived.

'The most emotional thing was actually going to the village and just walking around and thinking, "Wow, this is where my father's from. This is where my father's history is from." That was such a powerful thing. It reminded me of Alex Haley discovering his African ancestors in Roots. It was a blazing hot day, naturally bright sunshine, warmth. It just felt like the best feeling on earth.'

I try to imagine Joseph at twenty-five. Tipping up in some remote village in Nigeria, finding his long-lost father using nothing but his name and a faded photograph. Introducing himself. I'm stunned by the bravery of that, the sheer determination. I picture the sun beaming on Joseph's face as he drinks in the history, *his* history, and walks in his father's footsteps. I'm reminded that I don't know where in Jamaica my dad's parents are from. And I can't ask him.

'The fact that I have African history, without even knowing my father, has changed my life,' said Joseph. 'Without ever being present in my life, he has been a dramatic influence on my life, just because my experiences would have been totally different if I were white. That naturally leads to wanting to know more about your past.

'All my life up to that point, I knew my father was out there, but I didn't know anything about him. As I grew up, I needed to know what this half of me actually is about. And that desire just became more and more burning.

'My kids all have Igbo names because our heritage is from Eastern Nigeria. That was really important to me. It is an important part of our identity, even though it has not been as well known as I might have liked. Meeting my dad didn't work out exactly as I wanted it to, but I did eventually manage to track down my siblings, my half brothers and sisters, a few years ago, and that has been fantastic.'

Both Joseph's and Annalisa's stories show just how varied and unique mixed families can be. There isn't one picture-perfect portrait that can adequately reflect every mixed family, and as such, our experiences of growing up, parental support and wider familial interaction differ greatly. The impact of adoption, along with cultural mix, class, location and time-period, all provide an intricately unique web of experiences for each family. And, as Annalisa and Joseph have shown, the set-up and teachings of the family can create different perspectives for how mixed offspring see their position in the world.

For a long time, my own position in the world was impacted by a lack of connection with the Black side of my family. Like Annalisa and Joseph, my dad was brought up by someone other than his biological parents. And, just like them, I now find myself in my early adulthood searching for missing links to explain how and why I am who I am. Although it's on a completely different scale, and I have never travelled to a remote village on a different continent to track down a family member, I feel as though I can understand the urge to search for these biological connections; the feeling that it will help clarify aspects of my own identity. I know that in some cases, though, I have left that search too late.

My dad's father died before I mustered either the inclination or the courage to ask him any questions. The funeral was sad and strange. Carl died in the throes of cancer and dementia, a lethal combination that made it difficult for everyone around him in the final months of his life. He wasn't really so old, by today's standards, but he seemed to accept his fate in a way that shrunk him and made him frailer than you might expect. I don't call him my granddad because he was never that – but Dad had recently made peace with him and he wanted to be there, so we all went to the funeral.

My mum and sister travelled down in the morning from Manchester, my dad came down the night before, and I hopped on the Metropolitan Line from North London to Watford, home to Carl's daughter, dad's half-sister, my aunty, Sonya. The funeral was held in a church twenty minutes from her home, with a service in the function room of a pub down the road. Sonya, normally so matter-of-fact and straight-talking with an acerbic wit, sobbed as the casket was wheeled behind the curtain and my dad grabbed her arm. Carl was a father to her in a way he never was for my dad.

Carl stared at me from the sepia photo on the back of the service programme – dressed in a pristine white suit, posing hard, unsmiling, younger and stronger than I ever saw him. People I recognised only from a vast family Facebook group stood up and told stories about Carl. Stories about his impeccable dress sense, his love for his younger brother, his airs and graces and superior attitude. A woman I had never seen before cried as she choked through her eulogy, telling us how much she would miss his company, his humour, his kindness. I tried to connect anything anyone was saying to some kind of emotion in myself – but I couldn't, really. I was upset for Sonya, I was upset for my dad. I was upset at the missed opportunity for a connection, for the lost knowledge. I had assumed, naively and as we all do, that there would be time for all of that at some point. Our wilful overestimation of the time we are allotted is a human failing that dooms us all to heartbreak.

Carl lived in Kilburn, North-West London; practically around the corner from me in North London, where I've lived for the last eight years. But I never thought to go and see him, and he never contacted me. Well, that's not entirely true; in the last decade I saw him twice – and the first time was completely by accident.

I was in my second year of university and I was spending the summer teaching English at a school in the Basque country through an international programme that had been suggested by a tutor to enrich my learning and boost my CV. It was also paid, which was a big selling point for me. For some reason, my flight from Manchester to Bilbao involved a connection at Heathrow, which was entirely too much for nineteen-year-old me to handle. It was my first-ever solo flight and, inevitably, I missed my connection. As I stood, crying and pathetic, at the check-in desk, I realised I had one lifeline – my aunty Sonya. Angel that she is, she came to get me and whisked me back to her flat in Watford, as the next flight wasn't until the following morning. It also happened to be Father's Day.

'My dad's actually coming over for dinner,' said Sonya, shooting a worried look at me sideways as we flew down the motorway. 'Is that OK?'

'Oh! Erm . . . yes, of course!' I said enthusiastically, as my heart started to slowly contract. I kept my eyes on the motorway. What on earth would I say to this old man who I hadn't seen since I was a toddler? In my eyes, he abandoned my dad, showed no interest in me or my sister at any point in our lives, and I was pretty certain that he wouldn't want to see me now. But I knew Sonya would have warned him that I was there, and he still wanted to come over . . . Regardless, there was no way out of it.

When Sonya's front door banged shut, I sprang off my seat and stood weirdly to attention as Carl tottered, slightly unsteadily, into the living room. I gasped internally because he looked exactly like my dad, except old and miniature. I look a lot like my dad too; I wonder if Carl noticed that. There was a pause, an awkward hello, an even more awkward hug in which he pressed a £50 note into my hand, which I only half-heartedly attempted to give back (it felt weird accepting it, but I was also an impoverished student who now needed to pay for another flight to Bilbao).

The next time we met was voluntary. It was more than half a decade later and I was living in Archway, North London, working as a journalist. I had spoken to Sonya and decided that I wanted to meet him – on purpose this time. When I told my dad that I was meeting Carl, he promptly hung up on me, before calling me back almost immediately to apologise. He found the whole thing weird and hard. I did too, but it was important for me. I was an adult now, and my familial connections were no longer solely dictated by my parents. I wanted to at least reach out, even if I wasn't entirely sure why.

This time was less awkward. I wasn't a perpetually mortified teenager, which helped, and we had both had more time to mentally prepare. We sat on the sofa while Sonya made tea and snacks, and Carl pulled out an ancient photo album. He worked his way slowly through the pictures, pointing out my dad as a child in the 1970s, some pictures were of Becky and I, photos from the one visit we made to see him in London when we were babies – the only time Becky ever met him, and she was too young to remember. At the back of the book were newspaper clippings. Dad was a TV presenter; he read the news – ITV's *Granada Reports* – for seventeen years, and he had a seriously impressive career in journalism, particularly for someone who didn't go to university and only had two O Levels to his name. Carl had kept every article and interview that mentioned Dad, going back decades. He had cut them out neatly and glued them into this little book. He gave the book to me to keep.

Before Carl left, he whipped out his phone, an ancient-looking Nokia with huge buttons and pixelated picture display. He wanted to show me a photo of his bedside table. He spoke slowly and softly with a thick, unfamiliar Jamaican accent. I helped him pull up the photo from his phone gallery and zoom in. On each side of his bed were small, framed pictures of me and Becky; three in total. One from when we were very little; Becky a toothless, grinning cotton bud in a baby bouncer, me standing beside her in Tinkerbell pyjamas with enormous hair that formed a frizzy pyramid around my butter-wouldn't-melt smile. In the other two pictures we were school age — we wouldn't have seen him for years at that point — Becky in nursery, wearing a frilly dress, me gripping on behind her in my blue school jumper, hair now wrestled into two ridiculously thick plaits that stuck out at odd angles from my head. Those goofy grins were the last things he saw every night before he went to sleep. I didn't know how to feel. He wanted me to know that he hadn't forgotten about us, that him not being in our lives wasn't quite the straight cut-and-dry rejection I had always believed it to be.

Dad was brought up in care. His parents put him into foster care when he was just a few months old and never came back for him. He watched other kids come and go, staying weeks, months or years, but always eventually picked up by a blood relative. Dad was the only one who stayed. His foster mum was a white woman from Portsmouth, Audrey. She died the year I was born. Audrey is who my dad was referring to whenever he said 'Mum'. The woman who gave birth to him is Pauline. I have only a handful of vague memories of her before she moved back to Jamaica with her new husband when I was around eight. I remember she made the most delicious chicken I have ever tasted, she gave me goat's milk when I stayed with her, and she spoke like the Queen.

According to dad, the visits to Pauline were never very successful. There was the time she promised to spend a few days with us during the school holidays. Dad took time off work and planned an itinerary of fun activities – Becky and I were giddy as we hadn't seen her in years, but she only managed a couple of hours walking around the Trafford Centre with us. The next day she said she was too tired to see us, and she hopped on a train back to London with no further explanation. There was the time she invited Dad to the wedding of her new husband's son. Dad drove all the way from Manchester to Southampton only to discover that she was now not going to the wedding because of some argument, but hadn't bothered to let him know. And of course, there was the time when my mum discovered Pauline had been in the UK and hadn't told us or attempted to see us. They had been talking on the phone and Pauline had let something slip that she only would've known if she had been in the country – she tried to backpedal, but nothing gets past my mum.

I asked Dad about her recently – I don't know her, and I don't know much about her life, and I really want to believe that there's more to her not being in our lives than simple apathy. But Dad was stumped too. He couldn't tell me why she didn't come and get him when he was a kid, or why she didn't try harder to get to know her grandchildren. We know that she and Carl were first-generation immigrants trying to build a life in a hostile environment, and we know about the continuing trauma the Windrush generation has experienced at the hands of the British government. Their lives weren't easy or simple. Pauline has been living back home in Jamaica for more than twenty years. In the year before Dad died, he started talking to her again – at her request – for the first time in more than a decade. He told me that she mostly talked about the little trivialities of life in their phone calls: her new mobile phone, gossip about friends my dad didn't know. She wanted the slate to be wiped clean. I don't know if Dad ever gave her that, but he was able to give her twenty minutes of chat once a month in the final year of his life, which I think is as close to wiping the slate clean as he ever would have been able to get.

I thought about her as we left Carl's funeral. I thought about both of my estranged grandparents, and the family that Becky and I never got to know. To be clear, I'm not pinning this estrangement on the fact that we are an interracial family; their disconnection began way before Dad married a white woman, so it isn't that. But their actions created a barrier preventing Becky and I from meaningfully connecting with one side of our heritage – half of who we are. And I felt that loss keenly as we stood in a church full of strangers who looked like us.

One stereotype about interracial families is that we suffer from a lack of wider familial and social support. There is a perception that mixed families will be isolated because of judgement and disapproval, and that is obviously the case for some. One study even found that mixed children are less likely than non-mixed children to be close to their grandparents[7]; a finding which seems to perfectly nail the narrative of my own family story, or at least half of it. But I would argue that any isolation or disconnection that interracial families feel isn't necessarily a result of hostility, disapproval or racism – often

---

7   Cheng S, Powell B, 'Under and beyond constraints: Resource allocation to young children from biracial families', American Journal of Sociology, Vol. 112, Issue 4, January 2007

these families are disconnected simply due to geographical distance – and that, as with any relationship, it isn't always a permanent state of being, either.

Social scientist Remi Joseph-Salisbury argues that parents of mixed children are able to develop 'racial literacy, agency and resilience' to build their own social support structures[8]. His article, which focuses on Black mixed men in the UK and the US, found that mixed families are not the 'agency-less victims' they are often thought to be, and that rather than a place of instability or isolation, the family 'can offer an important site of support for Black mixed-race men as they move through a "post-racial" white supremacist society'.[9]

I see this racial literacy and resilience in my mum. She has spent the last few years reaching out to members of my dad's side of the family, building friendships and relationships, cultivating the connections that weren't given to us naturally. She has a deep understanding of how important those connections are for us and isn't afraid to put the work in to make that happen, for which I'm incredibly grateful. Some of Dad's family live in Manchester and meeting them has enriched my life. They are creatives, poets, theatre practitioners, public speakers. They are hilarious, kind, endlessly welcoming and earnestly interested in getting to know us.

These connections have become even more vital to me in the months since we lost Dad. They are a tether to him and his background, and I feel an urge to cling to them. I want to know everything about them and spend as much time with

---

8 Joseph-Salisbury, 'Black mixed-race men, perceptions of the family, and the cultivation of "post-racial" resilience', Ethnicities, Vol. 18, Issue 1, 2nd November, 2017
9 It's important to note that by focusing on males, Remi's article is highlighting the impact that gender has on the mixed experience.

them as I can. I don't want to stand at another funeral and wonder what I've missed out on.

The idea that the interracial family is doomed to isolation and a lack of support simply isn't true. Division and conflict can happen, as in any family, but that isn't an inevitable consequence of being in a mixed family and, when it does occur, the divisions aren't always irreparable. Look at Ciaran talking to his grandma about the British Empire and what she's learnt about racism in her pensioner history classes. Look at Joseph tracking down his father and his siblings, and giving his children names that reflect their Igbo heritage, and Annalisa vowing to find her birth parents before it's too late. Look at my dad attending the funeral of the man who offered him so little in life and, in his late fifties, deciding to connect with family members he had never spoken to before.

Negative social perceptions about mixed families persist on all sides of the racial spectrum, which can mean that even multicultural areas can feel isolating. But, at the same time, interracial families have the ability to overcome isolation and hostility through their fluidity and an innovative approach to developing alternative avenues of support[10]. Family constructs are ever-evolving, regardless of ethnicity, and for mixed families like mine, divisions do not define us.

Mum and Dad – Kim and Tony – were the inception point of our perfectly imperfect little family. They are our centre, our anchor, our point of belonging. But before they had my sister and I, they were a couple, they were in love. I often think of their resilience, their decision to persevere with their

---

10 Stephanie B. Guy, Yvonne Ayo, Roger Bullock, Dinah Morley, 'Breaking Stereotypes with Data: A Report on Mixed Race Children and Families in the UK', People in Harmony Research Report, 28th January, 2018

love despite the hostility faced by interracial couples in 1980s Britain. How have attitudes moved on today? And how are these relationship dynamics different for the mixed population? The ways in which we define our own identities within a family unit are so often dependent on how we understand and navigate the complexities of our own romantic lives and the unwieldy mechanics of falling in love.

# Chapter 3

# Love and Relationships

I was curious to explore how progressive attitudes towards interracial relationships in the UK really are. How might people feel when it's not just the couple down the road, but actually within their own family; their daughter or their grandson? Often, the thin façade of tolerance slips the moment something unfamiliar gets a little too close for comfort. For many people, bringing home a partner of a different race – to meet the parents, or even their friends – would still be 'a thing'.'

A 2012 report found that 15 per cent of people in the UK would be 'uncomfortable' if their child or grandchild was in a serious relationship or marriage with someone of a different ethnicity to their own. Twenty-three per cent said they were 'unsure' how they would feel about it. That's around a third of the population who would be likely to have a problem with an interracial relationship in their family – a significant proportion.

One in six people do not support marrying across 'racial lines'. One in four people aged fifty-five and over believe increased numbers of interracial relationships are a 'bad thing', and of all ethnic groups it was white people who showed the greatest opposition. Worryingly, opposition from younger groups was higher than you might expect, with one in five people aged 18–34 being against interracial relationships too.[1]

This opposition to interracial relationships is a transatlantic phenomenon, and more recent American studies have found similar responses. In 2016, research from the University of Washington concluded that some people who say they accept interracial marriage are masking deeper feelings of discomfort, even disgust[2]. The study found that bias against interracial couples is associated with a visceral reaction that ultimately leads interracial couples to be seen as *less than human*. Viewing pictures of interracial couples stimulated higher levels of activation in the insula – an area of the brain that controls the perception and experience of disgust.

In the 1990s, a survey found that disapproval of mixed marriages was at 40 per cent, but while more people today are likely to report that they are, in theory, 'comfortable' with interracial relationships, there is also the implication that many of those people are only OK with it if it's not in their backyard. Tellingly, in 2012, 13 per cent of the people who said that the growth of the mixed population was 'a good thing', also said they would *not* be comfortable if their child or grandchild was in a mixed relationship. If you think the mixed population is 'a good thing' as long as it's not in your own family, can you really think it's good?

Fast-forward eight years to current thinking. When Drake, the mixed-heritage Canadian rapper, revealed pictures of his

---

1  Rob Ford, Rachael Jolley, Sunder Katwala and Binita Mehta , 'The Melting Pot Generation: How Britain became more relaxed on race', British Future Research Report, 15th December, 2012

2  Allison L. Skinner, Caitlin M. Hudac, "'Yuck, you disgust me!" Affective bias against interracial couples', Journal of Experimental Social Psychology, Vol 68, January 2017

son Adonis in March 2020, a lot of the comments on Twitter, mostly from fans in the US and the UK, proved that disapproval and disgust at 'racial mixing' is still very much an issue.

One image was of Drake holding his blond, curly-haired little boy with Sophie Brussaux, his son's mother, who is reportedly also of mixed heritage, standing beside them. Beyond the endless jibes about Adonis' looks, his skin tone and hair colour (the joy of Twitter, where not even toddlers are safe from ridicule), there was also a barrage of tweets calling Drake a 'race traitor' and accusing him of 'diluting' his race. The criticism was thick, fast and came from all angles and people of all ethnic backgrounds, which leads me to believe that no matter who Drake ended up loving or starting a family with, he would always face contempt for making the 'wrong' choice.

Dating, falling in love and embarking on any new romantic relationship is, for everyone, a total emotional minefield. We throw ourselves, naked and vulnerable, into an ocean of other people's emotions, to be tossed around until we wash up, raw and choking, dry ourselves off, and jump in again. It almost feels like a form of madness. But there is hope with every jump. There has to be. *'This one will be different; this one will be the one.'*

How rare it is to find a meaningful connection with another person. To fall for someone at the same time as they fall for you. To navigate a person's unspoken intentions and hidden baggage and decide that all of that messiness will not only fit within your own life but will also somehow add to it. How rare for the timings, the circumstances, the feelings to be *just right* between two people to spark something that can last.

Finding love is even trickier now that our dating options have become as interchangeable and disposable as our

Deliveroo orders. Digitally, we are more connected than we have ever been, and the pool of prospective partners is deep and limitlessly accessible, and yet dating seems lonelier and more brutal than ever.

But when it works, nothing beats that feeling – the nerve-jolting, heart-skipping excitement of falling for someone. Really falling for someone. It's exactly that – a trip, a fall, an extra stair when you thought you had already reached the bottom. There is something essential and elementally human about this feeling. It's a reminder of our insecurity and fragility, a reminder that we are never as grounded as we think we are.

I say all of this with the heavy caveat that I have been in a relationship for the best part of a decade. My knowledge of modern dating has been gleaned vicariously through my single pals, greedily lapping up salacious tales of ghosting, experimental sexual encounters, meeting the friends then the parents for the first time, delicious first kisses, terrible first kisses. If I were to suddenly find myself single now, it would be like landing on a different planet. Tinder, Bumble, Hinge et al didn't exist when I met Jared. And as excited (and occasionally jealous) as my friends' stories make me, my overwhelming takeaway is still very much that dating is mostly hard and often cruel. And when you add a handful of different ethnic backgrounds and heritages into the mix, things only get harder, or, at least, more complicated.

Most discussions about ethnicity and dating – online, in the media, in dramas and novels – are centred around interracial dating, and almost overwhelmingly involve one partner who is white. There is rarely anything said about the dating experiences of mixed individuals, and there is limited research on how a mixed identity may influence the way you navigate romantic relationships.

It's almost a given that if you're mixed, you will end up in an interracial relationship – because even if you date another mixed person, it's unlikely you'll end up with someone with the *exact* same mix as you. So, a lot of the issues that crop up in discussions about interracial dating also apply to the mixed population. But there are some specific experiences in dating that are uniquely tied to being mixed – and they can make forging romantic connections complex. That said, complexity in relationships isn't necessarily something to be avoided.

When you're mixed, deciding who to date can feel weighted. Rather than a simple case of attraction that is unquestioningly accepted by the people in your life and the strangers you pass in the street, for mixed people, who you date can carry underlying assumptions about who you are and how you see yourself. This happens to monoracial people in interracial relationships too, of course. People make assumptions about anyone who dates a person of a different race, and some groups face more scrutiny than others.

One pervasive assumption that seems to be specific to the mixed experience is that choosing who to date equates to choosing a 'side'. It is as though your choice of romantic partner is your way of proclaiming to the world the element of your heritage you identify with the most, which is, obviously, a hopelessly simplistic and insulting framing of the situation. And yet it happens a lot.

As a mixed woman with a white partner, I have had it made abundantly clear to me by some that my choice of partner signi-fies that I have chosen whiteness as an identity. I've been called a 'race traitor' by trolls online, I've been accused of wanting to be white, I've been told that I can't authentically write about racism or racial discrimination because I have chosen the 'wrong side'. Some men – Black men – have, inexplicably, tried to use this assumption as a pick-up line. 'Why are you with him?' they have whispered as I passed them in a bar, Jared just out of earshot. 'You should be with someone like me.'

It works the other way too. When I've dated Black guys in the past, white men seem so much more wary of me. It's like I'm suddenly 'Blacker' in their eyes, more 'other', less approachable. They don't try to talk to me, they keep their distance. By dating a Black man, I have chosen Blackness – which is apparently an immediate red flag for some white men.

Who I choose to date is not a rejection of or an acceptance of any part of my racial heritage, it is really, truly, not that deep. In my experience, mixed people are not making meticulous, calculated decisions about who they love. And surely the whole concept of love is that it erodes your ability to make decisions – that you are powerless to its whims? It seems to be more the case that other people project their discomfort with our duality onto us, and that perpetuates this persistent need to believe that we are choosing sides and rejecting sides; as though to sit comfortably somewhere in between would be unimaginable. It's exhausting to have this additional weight of significance placed on your dating life by other people.

Judging someone's decision about who to love based on their ethnicity is rooted in sexual racism and is often informed by an underlying belief in racial purity, even if that belief is unconscious. 'Racial purity' sounds extreme, like a throwback to the brazen, violent racism of pre-civil rights-era America. But these attitudes still exist today and are held by people on both sides of the Atlantic. There is a lot of evidence to suggest that these archaic beliefs about preserving the 'cleanliness' of a bloodline by not 'mixing races' has been incubated through successive generations – just look at the hostility directed at

Drake's child, in 2020 – even if the end result is less openly hostile than it would have been a few decades ago.

So, mixed people face a kind of double whammy when it comes to love and dating. Not only are we a product of relationships that still have a worryingly high public disapproval rating, but we are also perpetuating this 'unsavoury' mixing, no matter who we choose to date. So, regardless of who we love, we're always going to piss somebody off. For some, me dating a white guy confirms to them that I am self-hating, rejecting my Black heritage and not equipped to speak on issues of mixedness or Blackness. For others, me dating a white guy is a dilution of the 'purity' of the white race. It's exhausting to be included in these shockingly reductive narratives, and it is genuinely concerning to know that so many people *still* think in such binary terms.

On the flipside of these problematic and damaging narratives is an acute awareness that dating, love and relationships will, in many ways, be easier for me to navigate than for some monoracial minority groups – because of the simple fact that I happen to have light brown skin.

Colourism, the privileging of light skin over dark skin within a minority group, dictates that mixed people with white heritage will be more successful in dating. There's a palatable 'exoticism' attached to having lighter skin that allows people to satisfy their curiosity without straying too far from the comfort of whiteness. It means mixed people with lighter skin will be deemed more attractive and more dateable by mainstream, Western hierarchies of beauty and desirability. Colourism isn't limited to skin colour, of course; it also includes hair texture, with straighter, smoother hair and looser curls pitched as more desirable then kinkier, coarser, more Afro-textured hair.

The privilege may not be across the board, and dating success is heavily dependent on many contextual factors, including what mix of ethnicities you are, how your physical features are perceived by others, where you happen to be in the world, and how you are defining 'success', but generally, in multicultural areas at least, mixed people have higher rates of dating success than monoracial minorities.

Research in 2015 that analysed the data of one of the largest US dating sites found that some multiracial people are preferred above *all* other groups – including white people.[3] The research, which analysed 6.7 million messages from the dating site, found that 'multiracial daters are treated very differently than single race daters, and, in fact, are afforded a preference premium in online dating'.

The study found that Asian-white women were viewed more favourably than any other group of women by both white and Asian men; Asian-white and Hispanic-white men were also preferred by Asian and Hispanic women respectively. But this effect wasn't consistent across all mixed groups.

For mixed Black-white multiracial daters, the picture is quite different. White men and women were still much *less* likely to respond to someone who identified as 'part Black and part white', than they were to another white person. However, Black-white multiracial daters received preferential treatment over their monoracial Black counterparts, who experienced the heaviest rejection in online dating – from everyone.

'In other words, Black women and men and White women and men respond more frequently to Black-White daters than

---

3 Celeste Vaughan Curington, Ken-Hou Lin, Jennifer Hickes Lundquist, 'Positioning Multiraciality in Cyberspace: Treatment of Multiracial Daters in an Online Dating Website', Vol. 80, Issue 4, 30th June, 2015

to Black daters, though they privilege Whiteness over Black multiraciality.' This suggests something more problematic is going on here.

This is an American study, and the US historically has quite a different dynamic with race and interracial dating than we do here in the UK, with different categorisations for different racial groups (for example, we would be less likely to refer to Hispanic as a 'race' in the UK), but the problematic nature of preference and rejection based on ethnicity undeniably exists here in the UK too.

What's striking, and depressingly unsurprising, about this study is that it is monoracial Black daters who are consistently at the bottom of the pile. This correlates with the findings of the well-known OK Cupid research from just a year before, which reported Black women receiving the lowest rating from all categories of online daters, closely followed by Black men.[4]

So, it makes sense that by proxy, Black-white mixed daters are less successful than mixed daters who don't have Black heritage. Any amount of Blackness appears to reduce your success as a prospective dater, and even trumps the relative dating advantages that come with mixedness. Could there be any clearer representation of white supremacy at work in the real world? The closer you come to whiteness, the more romantically appealing you are in the eyes of wider society – with Black people *always* at the bottom.

To exist somewhere around the midpoint on this sliding scale of supremacy is a strange place to be, particularly when it comes to romantic attention. I have felt men – specifically white men – grapple with their own discomfort when they stare at me, as though I represent some kind of forbidden fruit.

---

4  OK Cupid, 'Race and Attraction', 2009–2014

It manifests as a split-second flash of surprise in their expression, the furtiveness of their glances, a late-night confession that they always date 'girls like me' or else have never dated a 'girl like me'.

My sister and I felt it acutely two summers back on a long weekend in Budapest. We have built a tradition – my favourite tradition – in which we go to an obscure European music festival every year, as long as we like one artist on the line-up. We spend a day at the festival, and the rest of the trip we explore, bar-hop and seek out the sunshine. Last summer was Kaytranada in Lisbon, three years ago Jamiroquai in Aix-Les-Bains, France, and that summer we were seeing Arctic Monkeys at Sziget Festival in the Hungarian capital.

On a baking hot day, our last day in the city before flying home, Becky and I were exploring either Buda or Pest (we never figured out which was which) looking for somewhere to eat lunch. The food in Budapest was almost Bavarian with its salty, heavy meat stews and dumplings, and didn't lend itself to the cloying mid-August heat that bounced off the white stone tiles of pavement and clung to our skin. We kept moving, hunting for something lighter, cooler, a freezing glass of clear white wine with crisp salad, charcuterie, olives and cheese. We kept moving for another reason too: we could feel eyes on us.

Men working outside cafés attempting to reel in tourists, men working in bars and shops, men walking past us in twos and threes – they stared at us brazenly. We knew Eastern Europe wouldn't have the richest levels of diversity, but we didn't imagine we would stand out quite so obviously in the capital city, a metropolitan hub where so many of my white friends and colleagues had been for long weekends, hen dos, stag dos, never mentioning the complete lack of ethnic variety. But then, why would they notice? We noticed, though. On our visit, Becky and I saw hardly any other people of colour, and Black people were a particular rarity. We stood out, and the men we passed made sure to remind us of this.

This wasn't your average creepy staring that borders on street harassment. There was something different in their eyes, an unmistakeable undercurrent of hostility, laced with a weird spark of hunger. They assessed us from head to toe (making me wish I hadn't worn my smallest denim shorts), whispered to each other, sniggered unkindly, frowned or sneered – but they never took their eyes off us.

'They want to hate-fuck us,' Becky whispered to me when I asked her what the hell was going on. I laughed at my sister's ever-delicate phrasing, but her interpretation of their gaze was spot on. That's exactly what it felt like. They were looking at us as though they didn't know if they wanted to sleep with us or hurt us. It was an open hostility mingled with sexual attraction, or at least, sexual curiosity. It infuriated me to think we were being sexually and racially objectified like this, but Becky was able to shrug it off and laugh about it with ease. Soon she had me laughing about it too, with the help of that cool glass of white wine that we finally managed to find.

My sister always has great dating stories. I describe Becky to my friends as me, but funnier, which isn't strictly true. It *is* true that she's funnier than me, but that's not really the only way we're different. She feels things more intensely, she's more sensitive, more empathetic, moodier. But we have the exact same sense of humour, we love the same things, hate the same things. People struggle to tell our voices apart and our conversations are so quick and riddled with impenetrable in-jokes that it can sound like we're talking in code. We've been best friends from the moment she was old enough to become a willing accomplice in my mad games.

Dating and romantic attention has always been complicated for Becky. When she was younger, romance was tainted by low self-esteem and body image issues, which took her years to work through. In her mid-twenties, the façade of confidence that had been a front since her teens finally solidified and became real for her. Now, at thirty, she's closer to knowing who she is and what she wants than most people I know. And when it comes to dating, she's crystal clear on what she *doesn't* want.

'So, his Tinder bio said, "Black where it counts" with a laughing face emoji,' Becky told me. She was actually telling me this story for the second time, but I finally managed to record one of our calls after talking about it for weeks and failing to follow through. Becky lives in Manchester, where we grew up, so I don't get to see her anywhere near as much as I would like.

'I swiped right purely so I could give him a piece of my mind. He matched with me five minutes later. I immediately sent him a message that said, "FYI, your bio makes you sound ignorant, and racist as fuck. Laughing face."' Becky is nothing if not direct.

This particular Tinder charmer reacted surprisingly well to Becky's unapologetic dressing down. He messaged back immediately to say that he hadn't realised his bio came across like that, that he had just found it funny. In the next breath he asked Becky out on a date, so she unmatched him. But it doesn't always go as smoothly as this, and she often finds herself dealing with angry or defensive responses, or people just ghosting her – even when she calls things out really gently – so it's not always worth the emotional effort.

'In maybe 40 per cent of all my dating interactions, race

comes up in some way or another. Often, whatever they say is intended to be taken as a compliment. I think a lot of these guys – and it's almost all white guys that I'm speaking to on Tinder – seem to think that it's what I want to hear.'

Becky told me men on dating apps will often get overtly sexual with her very quickly. She says it makes her second-guess herself and question her own behaviour. Is she doing something to trigger this forwardness in guys? Is she asking for it?

I suggest it could be to do with the 'Jezebel' stereotype. This is an outdated and offensive portrayal of Black women as hypersexual, promiscuous, insatiable – we see it again and again in popular media, films, music videos, advertising and literature. The Jezebel stereotype is a way of distorting and dehumanising Black women, of objectifying their bodies and their sexuality in order to undermine and devalue their experiences of love and romantic relationships. This stereotype, which implies that Black women are more likely to be up for casual sex or 'dirtier' sexual acts, is an intrinsically anti-Black image that purposefully contrasts with the purity and chastity historically associated with white women. It can also make romantic interactions fraught and hostile for Black and mixed women.

While this negative trope is thought to pre-date the transatlantic slave trade, the long-term implications of viewing Black women in this way still persist today. A 2018 study conducted in Australia revisited the Jezebel stereotype and found that this form of sexual objectification still impacts how Black women are perceived in modern society. They found that people spend more time looking at the sexual body parts of Black women than they do of white women, and that Black women are 'implicitly associated to both animals and objects to a greater degree than White women'.[5] They added that these assumptions are so ingrained that this kind of sexual objectification often happens 'outside the realms of conscious thought' – meaning that people frequently hypersexualise Black women without even being aware that they are doing it.

Becky told me that it is something she frequently feels projected onto her by the white men she talks to on Tinder. Although she might experience this hypersexualisation with less frequency and in different ways than darker-skinned Black women, Becky's experiences suggest that this stereotype applies to Black women of all skin tones, Black mixed women included.

'Obviously, being ghosted or ignored after a date is really standard, I've done it to guys myself, but I do wonder sometimes, when I don't hear back from someone after a date, whether it's because they had an expectation about me that I wasn't aware of. Sometimes I think being mixed means I can get more matches on Tinder, but less substance.'

These unspoken expectations, and the assumptions that she will be instantly up for sex, make dating exhausting for Becky. She's sick of the outdated, belittling comments about the colour of her skin, men's obsession with her 'otherness', the way she is reduced to something edible, something to be consumed, constantly referred to as 'caramel', 'chocolate' or 'honey'. She is exasperated that after about ten years of dating, she is still having the same conversations with men.

'I spoke to my therapist about the fact that I find it hard to take compliments. I think part of that stems from an uncertainty about where the compliment is coming from.

---

5  Joel Anderson, Elise Holland, Courtney Heldreth, Scott Johnson, 'Revisiting the Jezebel Stereotype: The Impact of Target Race on Sexual Objectification', Psychology of Women Quarterly, Vol. 42, Issue 4, August 2018

'I've taken "compliments" before, and when I think about some of them now, I would love to go back and slap a guy right in the face for saying it. Now, I'm more prepared. But that also means I'm more defensive and more ready to be offended. It definitely adds an additional level of stress to dating.'

When I think about some of the things men say to Becky on dating apps, my big-sister instinct kicks in and I feel my blood boil. Beyond the anger, it also reminds me how far removed my own experiences of love and relationships are. As I mentioned, I have never had to navigate the modern world of digital dating. Now, in my early thirties, having been in a relationship for the best part of a decade, my experience of falling in love and navigating new romantic relationships as an adult is woefully limited. My experience of being in love, however, is incredibly rich.

I was twenty-three when I met Jared. I had been living in London for just six months. I still wore my hair relaxed and fried straight, with a noughties-era sweeping side fringe. It was a chilly March evening, and we were standing outside a pub in West London when we said our first words to each other. I don't remember what they were. I was wearing too much bronzer, a navy blue dress that was both short and low-cut, and wedged metallic heels. I didn't wear coats on nights out back then. He was tall and blond with green eyes, he was wearing something grey, a hoodie, I think, and a beanie hat. I took a sip of my cheap white wine, which I thought made me look classy and aloof, and internally resolved to take him home that night.

I fell in love with Jared slowly, but still quicker than he fell in love with me – he is meticulous in his decision making, sometimes infuriatingly so. He likes to be sure, really sure, before diving in. I'm more impatient, decidedly less considered, and I got there first, resulting in a torturous few months during which I wasn't sure if he would jump to meet me. But he did. And around nine months in, on my birthday, he told me that he loved me as we sat on my bed in my flat-share in North London, a dilapidated duplex directly above a greasy spoon café, so close to the Emirates Stadium we could hear the Arsenal players being announced onto the pitch on Saturday afternoons.

A born-and-bred Londoner, Jared laughed at me when I tried to get black cabs, taught me which tube stations were actually quicker to walk between, introduced me to the best restaurant in Chinatown (Wong Kei), and the only place to get cheap lunch in Soho (Gaby's). He was a walking cheat-sheet to this complicated city and made me hopeful for the first time since I had moved that I might be able to make this place my home. His friends were actors, dancers, theatre makers, creatives . . . and they were all overwhelmingly extroverted, warm and welcoming. We spent our weekends watching plays at The National, The Bush, The Almeida, The Donmar, watching independent and classic films at the British Film Institute and the Prince Charles Cinema, getting wasted and dancing until 3 a.m. at hip hop and R&B nights at Concrete and The Book Club in Shoreditch.

I couldn't help but fall in love with Jared. He is one of the kindest people I have ever met, with a rare determination to see good in everyone. His brightness balances my natural leaning towards the dark and takes the edge off my cynicism. It's a love that made me realise that I hadn't been in love before. Not properly. And the stakes are so high. Every screaming row or tearful argument in those first few years had an undercurrent of pure terror – an abject fear of losing it all. But I took comfort in the fact that Jared was afraid too. We shook the fear from each other every time we made up, each pulling the other back to a place of delicate, quivering hope.

I've never been in a relationship for anywhere near this long before, and the ferocity of my feelings now is, if anything, stronger than in the beginning. To be told that this love, this great love, this love of my life, has anything to do with a desire to be closer to whiteness, makes absolutely no sense to me. That is what is being implied when I get messages online from people asking me why I have a white boyfriend, or a whispered insistence that I have chosen the 'wrong side'. This isn't a love that can be diluted so easily, watered down with these basic assumptions. In today's world, no one should have to explain or justify who they love simply because of their race.

To be clear, this doesn't happen often. When Jared and I walk down the street holding hands, it's incredibly unlikely that we will face any open hostility, looks or comments. In the nine years we have been together, I can count the instances of anything like this happening on one hand. We live in London and there are much more interesting and controversial things to look at than us. As for the online stuff, as a journalist writing about racism, I put myself in the firing line for these comments much more than most. But, even if my exposure to these attitudes is disproportionate, it still flags the fact that they are out there. Like so much of the racial hostility in this country, it is the things that *aren't* said that are often the most dangerously pervasive; the views hidden behind closed doors that occasionally spill over into everyday microaggressions or are given the space to thrive in online anonymity.

But what of love and relationships beyond the millennial experience? What are the experiences of older members of the mixed population, those who met and fell in love before

Tinder was a thing? Those who have navigated love, dating, marriages, families, in a time when hostility towards interracial relationships was much more brazen, when meeting a lover's family or simply holding hands in public was more difficult, more dangerous, than it is now.

Mel is fifty-six and she works as a business coach and consultant. Her late father is Black Jamaican, her mother is white English, although Mel says her mother actually identifies as Cornish, not English. Her experiences of dating and relationships as a young woman were shaped by her upbringing in 1970s rural England, and the political context that informed public attitude at the time.

She was a military kid. Her parents met in the Royal Air Force and Mel was born in Libya, where they were stationed at the time. She spent the first few years of her life in Gibraltar and the family moved around a lot – to different RAF bases – until they finally settled in a village in East Anglia when Mel was around ten years old.

'Although I grew up in a very white, rural area of England in the 1970s, in our little village, unusually, there were two other mixed families. We also lived next door to a black American military family, because they were stationed there too.' I was speaking to Mel on Zoom during the December lockdown of 2020, and it was nice to see a new face. Mel has a similar light skin tone to my own, kind eyes and a wide smile. She looks much younger than her age and looking at her reminds me how rarely I meet people who look like future versions of myself.

'I grew up in a diverse, mixed world at home, which was so rare for the time and the fact that I was in the countryside. I have lots of memories of everyone hanging out and having parties and playing rounders and having a great time.

But when I was at school, I was very much in the minority.'

When Mel was a teenager and a young adult, mixedness wasn't presented as cool or attractive, as it is now. The contemporary studies that have found mixed people have greater success in dating, and that our features are covetable and desired, didn't apply back then. Mel was seen simply as 'other', and frequently made to feel unwelcome, unattractive and undesirable.

'I came home from school one day crying, I must have been around thirteen at the time, because a boy had used the N word. The boy refused to sit next to me, and he called me the N word. There were lots of things like this that would have been called "teasing" at the time but would now be called bullying and racism. At five years old, I was washing my hands at school and a little boy asked me, "Does it come off?" That was the moment I became Black in a sense, the moment my consciousness opened up to my difference.

'The racism that I experienced at the time was being endorsed by the media, endorsed by politicians. The Tory government was really fanning the flames of racism; I think they still are, actually. The National Front was gaining influence, a boy who sat behind me at school would always talk about how they were going to win power – I was terrified by that.'

As Mel tells me this, I remember that Enoch Powell's infamous and offensive 'Rivers of Blood' speech would have happened while Mel was a child. The brazenness of this level of open hostility and racism – from elected officials – is hard to comprehend for someone who was born twenty-odd years later.

'Back then, nobody said I was mixed race. I was Black. There was never any real distinction made,' explained Mel.

'Now, I politically identify as Black, but I am also very proud of my mixed-race identity. I see mixed race as a particular way of being Black, and I do think it is a different and specific experience. You are, whether you like it or not, at the intersection of two different conversations, and sometimes two different cultures.

'I used to feel ashamed of being part white because the more I understood the history, the more I wanted to deny that part of me. I felt so angry. But, as I matured, I realised that I didn't want to deny my mother, or my cousins, who I love. I used to feel as though I didn't belong anywhere, but then the more I grew into my maturity, and the more work I did on personal development, I began to realise that I belong everywhere.'

This deep understanding of and confidence in her place in the world has helped Mel navigate different romantic relationships throughout her life. She told me that although she can only speak on her own experiences, she thinks being mixed makes you more open to difference, by nature of who you are and your family experiences.

'I have dated men from all backgrounds. Black, brown and white. I would say that if you're in a relationship with someone who's white – that can be a romantic relationship, but also with white family members – they are never ever going to understand what it feels like to experience racism.

'There is a kind of gap there, compared to when I have had partners who were Black or brown. Non-white romantic partners just have this understanding of some of the things that you have to deal with. But even then, I have never dated anyone who is mixed race, so nobody I have been with has ever understood what I deal with as a mixed person. It can put you in a lonely space. Although I am close to my sister and mixed-race friends who, of course, fully understand.'

An important caveat for Mel when she has dated white men in the past is that there has to be a lot of conversation about ethnicity, a frequent sharing of experiences and, most importantly, a willingness to listen and learn.

'I would never date a white person who wasn't interested in understanding my experiences, or wasn't interested in learning more about racism, because that would just be such hard work,' she added. Luckily that hasn't been a problem for the last two decades of her life.

Mel's husband is a white Danish man named Peter, and she has been with him for twenty years. She describes him as 'clued up' and says that even though he doesn't have the lived experiences she does, she and Peter are able to talk about ethnicity and racism with a frankness and mutual honesty that brings them closer together.

'He might not always understand why something has upset me. Certainly, he can understand it intellectually, but he doesn't experience the emotions that I might go through,' said Mel. She was considered and slower with her words while she told me this, as though it was something she hasn't needed to ask herself for a long time.

'I find him to be a very open and unprejudiced person. I wouldn't marry somebody who wasn't. What I really like about him is that he's willing to talk about these issues, and he's not worried about being politically correct. He will talk about difficult subjects, and if he doesn't understand something, he will ask the questions and do the work to figure it out.'

But it hasn't always been plain sailing. Before meeting Peter, Mel had to navigate all kinds of issues with white partners. More often than not, it wasn't the person she was dating who caused problems, but their families and wider circles.

'When I've had white partners, they never ever think that race is an issue. I'm the one that goes into the relationship thinking, "I wonder how they think" and "I wonder how their families think." I have had issues where parents have said dodgy things. And that has been uncomfortable. Usually, they are incredibly nice people, they love you and what they're saying isn't directed at you – but that doesn't make it less hurtful. A close relative of a white guy I was dating said something negative about African countries not being able to govern themselves. That really upset me. I didn't say anything at the time. Nowadays, I would have, but then, I felt I had to just swallow the fury.'

But, for all the fury, the discomfort and the uncertainty that Mel has felt over the years, and the racism and hostility she has faced as a child and as a young woman, Mel is overwhelmingly proud of who she is. And, at fifty-six, she has found a certainty in her own identity, and holds the firm belief that being mixed is a 'gift'.

'I feel I am evidence of the inevitable exchange between different people in life. I'm not one of those people who thinks everyone should mix so we all end up coffee-coloured. I think we need difference. We need white people; we need very dark Black people. We need all of the difference available. And we need to allow people who are a mixture of those things.

'When Peter and I got married, we invited our friends and our family, and it was so diverse. It was just phenomenally colourful and vibrant, with people from so many different parts of the world, so many different skin tones. Peter's mother said afterwards, "This is how the world should be", and that brought tears to my eyes. I remember thinking, "Yes, this is this is how the world *could* be."'

For Mel, one of the most important things in her marriage has been the ability to communicate, to talk about lived experiences, to bridge that inevitable gulf of understanding. Jared and I spoke about ethnicity and racism early and often. He grew up in North London, in incredibly diverse circles – far more so than mine – so he had had all of the important conversations and necessary revelations way before I came on the scene. I'm not the only Black or mixed woman he has dated, nor does he have a 'thing' for women who look like me. We are lucky in that our politics align and have done since the beginning. We wouldn't have lasted this long if they didn't. Without this implicit understanding and ability to communicate fluidly and effectively about these issues, I can't imagine a relationship ever truly being able to flourish.

Alexander agrees with this. As a young gay man, Alexander has a perspective on dating, love and relationships that I will never be able to experience. Alexander is Sri Lankan and British, but he was born and grew up in Australia. Now, he lives in London, and like Becky, is experiencing the full spectrum of highs and lows that come with modern, digital dating, but he says talking about ethnicity, mixedness and interracial dynamics is always a priority when he is interacting with someone new.

'I don't give people the benefit of the doubt and I don't try to educate people. I already do enough of that in my life,' he told me. We met in an East London café to drink herbal tea and talk relationships. Alexander is tall and broad with light skin and deep brown eyes. This was only the second time we had met, but the warmth in his voice and smile made me feel as though we had known each other for much longer. I imagine he has a similar effect on dates too.

'If it happens with a work colleague or a stranger at a

party, it might be a slightly different conversation. I might feel inclined in that particular context to explain why a comment is offensive or problematic or racist, but in my dating life, I'm looking for someone I can connect with, someone I can be vulnerable with. If that person is coming at you from the get-go with preconceived ideas about who you are, or who they want you to be based on the way that you look, I don't think that is someone who is worth pursuing.'

Alexander doesn't always mind having these awkward conversations with prospective love interests – he knows that they have to happen eventually – but he never wants it to be the focal point of their initial interactions; he feels that's really important in forming something lasting. As we drained the last of our tea and felt the day darken outside, our conversation turned more personal, and Alexander told me he was currently seeing someone – a mixed guy. He explained that he has never dated anyone mixed before, at least not on a long-term basis, and he said it was in some ways like a breath of fresh air.

'When we spoke about our heritage, it wasn't a conversation that was had in a self-conscious way. It was a conversation that came from a place of shared understanding and curiosity. I don't really know how to explain it. It's just that I felt like I could talk about that stuff without feeling uncomfortable, or judged, for the first time.'

He says that not having to go through the rigmarole of carefully explaining his heritage and unpicking his background to appease someone else's curiosity is a huge relief. It makes him feel instantly closer to that person; it's a signal that he can truly be himself, an interpersonal understanding on a level he said he hasn't experienced in a romantic partner before. I have never dated someone who is mixed, but I can see the appeal of this – the simplicity and ease of an unspoken, mutual understanding.

'When you do have that experience with someone, especially in a romantic setting, it's really disarming, but in a good way. It's empowering to know that person will just get it. It reminds me that the awkward interactions I've had dating in the past don't have to be the norm. I want to protect that. It's important.'

This conversation was months ago now, and I wonder if this relationship endured, or if it fizzled. I got the feeling Alexander liked this guy. He was coy talking about him, almost as though he didn't want to jinx anything. I know that feeling; the tentative fear when the stakes start to climb. I hope it worked out for them. And if not, I hope he's willing to jump back in.

Jumping into the world of love and relationships is never easy, and it takes courage and conviction. This plunge can be particularly tricky when you don't know quite what it is that the other person likes about you. In recent years, a certain kind of 'mixed aesthetic' has become popularised in mainstream and social media. Certain 'mixed features' have now become so coveted that it can be hard to differentiate a genuine, organic attraction from a problematic racial fetish.

# Chapter 4

# Exoticisation, Fetishisation and Othering

Something strange happens when I'm told that I'm beautiful. Depending on who is saying it, I sometimes feel an instinctive mistrust, an underlying questioning of where that compliment is coming from. And it's a feeling that's deeper than simply struggling to take a compliment. So often, comments on my appearance are laced with things that don't sound quite so complimentary when you pick them apart – 'exotic' for example – and they remind me that the current and relatively recent fixation on 'mixed features' as a standard of beauty is inherently problematic.

I understand this a lot more clearly now than I did when I was a teenager. Back then, in the noughties, mixed models weren't plastered all over billboards and TV adverts, influencers weren't tanning their skin, plumping their lips and curling their hair to look like me. When I was at school, and even university, I wouldn't really believe people if they told me I was beautiful. How could I when I didn't look like any of the beautiful people I saw on TV or in the movies? Or when my hair didn't swish when I turned my head? How could I believe I was beautiful when they would also tell me that my bum was too big, my lips were too much, my hair was too frizzy? Back then, they didn't talk about my looks in a covetous way; there was no implication that anyone actually wanted to look like me – it was a 'beauty' that they liked to observe, to comment on, to dissect, but always from a safe distance.

I spent my late childhood and teens in this state of uncertainty about my appearance. Like many awkward teenagers, my deepest desire was to conform, to blend in, to look exactly like everyone else. My biggest fear was being singled out from the crowd for any reason at all. Individualism was the antithesis of everything fourteen-year-old Natalie wanted to be. It was about acceptance; I wanted to be absorbed into the masses, consumed by them, be told I was one of them. It's a common malaise for teenagers, this near-crippling insecurity as you work to figure out who the hell you are, but looking back, I know there was an edge to my experience of this feeling. Being mixed in largely white environments definitely intensified my need to fit in.

'It's tingling now,' I manage to pipe up after finally mustering the courage to speak. The hairdresser I'm talking to – now knuckle-deep in another woman's box braids – glances over at me and says simply, 'Not yet.'

I swallow and set my eyes on the music video playing on the TV screen positioned high on the wall above the salon door. I can't hear it over the hairdryers, but I know Ciara is singing about her 'goodies', her poker-straight, silky hair bouncing on her shoulders as she hits that complex choreography. I stiffen my resolve. Tingling had actually been an understatement. The relaxer on my scalp is burning now. A blob has fallen onto my ear and it's agonising, but I'm scared to wipe it off in case the hairdresser sees me messing with it. So I sit there and try to mentally twist the pain into something positive, transformative. The deeper the pain, I tell myself, the more I will look like Ciara, or my friends at school, when they eventually rinse this stuff off my head.

'Relaxer' is a misnomer. There is violence to the process. A relaxer is a powerful chemical in a lotion form that reduces the curl by breaking down the hair strand and chemically altering the texture. It can result in serious breakage, stunted hair growth and chemical burns. The process strips your hair of its natural oils, making it fragile and brittle. It also makes the hair easier to manage and I was more than willing to risk irrevocable damage for a shot at conformity.

The results vary depending on your hair texture, but for me – with my combination of 3c/4a curls – the process smoothed the hair enough that I could straighten it to within an inch of its life with my industrial-grade GHDs. It was 2005 after all and poker-straight hair was the in-thing, along with brutally butchered eyebrows, heavy pencil eyeliner and low-ride skinny jeans.

My Year Eleven prom was looming, and I had finally convinced my mum to let me get my hair relaxed. She had always vehemently protested and had been the biggest champion and admirer of my curls since I could remember, but there is an impermeable quality to compliments that come from your own mother; they rarely sink in. My teenage will was strong and disruptive, and Mum buckled eventually. We drove to Moss Side, just a stone's throw from the white suburb in south Manchester where we lived, found the Black hair salon that had been recommended by a family friend and paid around £100 for the treatment and a trim (something I would find the money to keep doing every four to six months for the next eight years).

My hair didn't want to be straight. It fought back, snapped off, turned straw-like in protest. But I didn't care. Every morning, smoke billowed from our living room as my sister and I burnt our curls into submission with our straighteners – our aim: to fry as close to the root as we could stand. The hot, searing smell was comforting to us. At that time, even a poor imitation of my white friends' hair was preferable to me than my unmanageable frizz.

It took a long time, but this attitude finally started to fade as I got older and grew more confident and less reliant on validation from others. I moved to London in my early twenties and was confronted with more diversity than I had ever seen. In this city there wasn't only one way to be beautiful. People weren't striving for conformity; they were striving to forge their own identities. It felt like a collective of individuality and I fell in love with it. I marvelled at the Black and mixed women I saw on the tube with braids twisted up with bright blue or lilac; intricate cornrows snaking the circumference of their scalps, huge, buoyant Afros alive with kinetic energy. They were undeniably beautiful and glowing with confidence, and they made me feel brave simply by being in their presence. I stopped straightening my hair; I didn't need to any more.

Along with my skin tone, my tightly coiled curls have always been the most obvious physical marker of my Blackness, and I battled to suppress it for much of my youth. That's still a painful thought. Hating something about yourself isn't inherent, so where had I learnt that? Teaching myself to love my hair felt like an awakening. It was more than just a hairstyle change, it was an acknowledgement of who I really am, and a conscious decision to present myself openly and proudly to the rest of the world. Better late than never.

But as I reached my mid-twenties, I began to feel a shift in beauty standards that spread beyond the boundaries of London.

Suddenly, there were faces like mine on every other advertising campaign, white women were sporting deeper, darker tans, lip fillers and bum implants, on social media. Suddenly it felt as though the features I had tried to hide or dilute in my teens were now covetable, desirable. I couldn't understand how or exactly when this shift had happened. How is it that mixed people are now, in this cultural moment, perceived as beautiful, when that didn't seem to be the case for so much of my early life? How did it become trendy to be mixed?

A 2018 study in the *Journal of General Psychology* found that faces of 'mixed racial phenotypes' are perceived as more attractive than stereotypically white and Black faces[1]. In the study, researchers had hundreds of undergraduate students rate the attractiveness of computer-generated faces that varied in racial features and skin tone. Consistently, participants rated mixed faces with 'medium' skin tone as the most attractive. This study was only concerned with Black/white mixed individuals, but it is something that is found consistently among other kinds of mixes, too.

A 2010 study in the journal *Perception*, found that 'people of a mixed Asian and European background were rated as more attractive than Asians [and] Europeans.'[2] Asian-white women get the most attention on online dating apps compared to women who publicly identified as only white or only Asian[3].

---

1 Elena V. Stepanova, 'Attractiveness as a Function of Skin Tone and Facial Features: Evidence from Categorization Studies', Journal of General Psychology, Vol. 145, Issue 1, November 2017
2 Michael B. Lewis, 'Why are Mixed-Race People Perceived as more Attractive?', Perception, Vol. 39, Issue 1, 1st January 2010
3 Celeste Curington, Ken-Hou Lin, Jennifer Lundquist, 'Dating Partners Don't Always Prefer "Their Own Kind": Some Multiracial Daters Get Bonus Points in the Dating Game', Council on Contemporary Families Briefing Paper, 1st July 2015

Interestingly, another study from 2018 found that when Black people were labelled as 'mixed race', they were perceived as more attractive, even though they weren't actually mixed[4]. This seems to make it clear that the idea of an inherent mixed beauty standard is loaded with centuries of conscious and unconscious racial bias. Perceiving mixed people – specifically people who are mixed with whiteness – as beautiful is more about power and racial hierarchies than it is about how we actually look.

Deeply entrenched in modern mixed beauty ideals is the concept of colourism. I mentioned colourism in Chapter 3, Love and Relationships, but this specific form of racism is incredibly relevant to concepts of beauty and fetishisation too. It all comes down to proximity to whiteness. The closer you are to whiteness – in a visual sense – the more likely you are to be positioned as beautiful. Colourism is the preferential treatment of those with lighter skin and the denigration of those with darker skin, and it is often perpetuated by people *within* minoritised ethnic groups, as well as white people. The roots of colourism stem from the hierarchies of white supremacy, and it is the reason why people who look like me are currently celebrated for our looks, when darker skinned Black people and other darker-skinned minorities are not.

Colourism and skin tone affect everything from dating and desirability to job prospects. A 2007 study found there to be a difference in pay rates between darker-skinned and lighter-skinned men.[5] Dark-skinned girls are three times as likely to be

---

4   Robert L. Reece, 'What are you mixed with: The Effect of Multiracial Identification on Perceived Attractiveness', The Review of Black Political Economy, Vol. 43, Issue 2, January 2016
5   Arthur H. Goldsmith, Darrick Hamilton and William Darity Jr, 'From Dark to Light: Skin Color and Wages among African-Americans', The Journal of Human Resources, Vol. 42, 1st September, 2007

suspended from school than their lighter-skinned classmates.[6] The unsettling insistence of the superiority of mixed beauty only fuels this damaging narrative.

My lighter skin tone has afforded me buckets of privilege and open doors in comparison with my darker-skinned friends and family members. And it isn't only skin tone that plays into this phenomenon; colourism also covers hair texture and even your facial and physical features (sometimes colloquially dubbed 'featurism'), with those who fall closer in line with Eurocentric beauty standards afforded more privilege than those who do not. It's an unpleasant reality of a society still operating on the basis of white supremacy. Opportunities shouldn't be offered on a sliding scale depending on ethnicity, skin tone or any other superficial quality, but this is currently the world we live in, and it's on all of us, no matter where we fall on the scale, to recognise it, call it out wherever we see it, and push back against it.

People like me, who 'benefit' from the system, need to use their position of relative privilege to acknowledge the existence of this unfair, regressive hierarchy, and do what we can to support and speak up for our darker-skinned and monoracial peers. It's also important to remember that the apparent privileges that come with being at the lighter end of the colourism scale are tainted and riddled with caveats; the benefits afforded to us are fleeting, superficial and only handed out by those who will always hold more power. When it comes to equality, no one wins unless we all win.

---

6   Lance Hannon, Robert DeFina, Sarah Bruch, 'The Relationship Between Skin Tone and School Suspension for African Americans', Race and Social Problems, Vol. 5, December 2013

★

With so much of my so-called 'beauty' wrapped up in my proximity to whiteness – the 'caramel' skin, the looser curls, the slimmer nose, the watering down of my visible markers of Blackness – it is no surprise that mixed people who don't fit this mainstream blueprint of mixedness, those with darker skin or no white heritage, have a different experience of beauty and being fetishised or othered. This is definitely the case for Aziza, who has direct experience of colourism levelled at her from within her own family.

Aziza is a fashion and lifestyle blogger who lives in London, but her family hail from Africa and the Middle East. Her mother's side is from Oman and her father's side is from Zanzibar, a small island off the eastern coast of Africa. She tells me she has struggled with the concept of beauty since she was a child.

'The anti-Blackness in Arab communities is usually to do with skin colour – people with darker skin tones are definitely treated differently,' explained Aziza. She has glossy skin, darker than mine, deep brown eyes and dark, shoulder-length curly hair. The light pink knit jumper she was wearing on the day we met made all that rich melanin gleam.

'If you ask anyone in our family, my grandmother is always classed as the epitome of beauty and everyone will tell you this. Why? Because my grandmother – she is also called Aziza – is of a very fair complexion and has these amazing green eyes,' she told me.

She may be her namesake, but that is where the similarities end for Aziza and her grandmother. For her grandmother to be lauded as the family's great beauty, specifically because of her fairer features, sent a clear message to young Aziza – that beauty is intrinsically linked to lightness, something she would never be able to achieve naturally.

Growing up, Aziza was told to hide from the sun as much as possible, and this message came from both sides of her family: 'Even my dad's mother, who is a proud African woman, would tell me not to go out in the sun too much because I would get "too dark", and I always thought, what does that even mean? There is no such thing as too dark.'

Having been brought up in the UK, Aziza has a completely different relationship with the sun. She loves to tan. She finds it jarring when she goes to Oman and everyone is hiding from the rays. But the lengths people will go to in order to meet the culturally decided standards of beauty are shocking. The popularity of skin lightening creams all over the world are testament to the pervasive, global messaging that lighter is better. When you're mixed, there is an expectation that you will be lighter, less obviously 'other'. That's what makes us palatable and acceptably attractive to the masses. But there is no blueprint for how any mixed person will look, and if, like Aziza, you don't meet those expectations, navigating how people respond to you can be tricky.

'Fair and Lovely is a skin lightening brand, and it is a huge thing in Oman,' said Aziza. She told me that her mum gave her one of the creams to use when she was younger and that she hadn't known what it was or what it would do to her skin.

'I was using it on my face. When Mum gave it to me, I thought it was just getting rid of blemishes. I thought it was just a face wash. But the cream was really strong and it stung my eyes. That's when I looked into it and realised what I was using. Yes, my blemishes were fading, but it was doing more than that. It would attempt to make me lighter, but I felt that no one had made that clear to me.'

Aziza is an influencer with thousands of followers on Instagram. Beauty and aesthetics are a big part of that. Her profile is bold colours, statement outfits and cute head-tilt selfies. On the face of it, she hardly looks lacking in self-confidence about her appearance, but growing up it was a different story entirely. She says living in London has allowed her to accept and celebrate who she is.

'All the women that you see on TV in Arab countries have light skin, they dye their hair blonde, they wear light contacts. I'm really happy to live where I live. If I was living in Oman, most likely I would have really long, straight hair, I would probably be using lightening creams and always complaining about hyper-pigmentation, worrying that I wasn't light enough,' she says.

Despite having darker skin than many of her family members, Aziza is conscious that she still holds relative privilege outside of that sphere. She recognises herself as 'darker-skinned' in terms of colourism in Asian and Arab communities, but not in comparison to dark-skinned Black women who will face more oppression because of their skin tone.

'I have the features that I have, and I am who I am,' Aziza adds. 'In the UK we have a long way to go, but we do have a lot more mainstream representation than other countries. I grew up with role models, seeing women who looked like I do in the media and in advertising. That was so important for me, for building my confidence.'

At the moment, advertisers seem to be cooperatively pushing the same agenda – that it is cool and attractive to be mixed – and they are increasingly using mixed families to tick that box. The last few years have seen an explosion of interracial families featuring in TV adverts. John Lewis, Morrisons, Marks and Spencer and H&M are just a handful of the giant corporations that have featured a mixed family in a major campaign. In 2015, only 5.65 per cent of British ads featured Black people, 3.86 per cent people of mixed-ethnicity, and 2.71 per cent of Asian descent[7]. So, this sudden influx of non-white faces in mainstream ad campaigns is a significant change and it is easy to see this as a major step towards better inclusivity and representation. Like Aziza says, there is certainly value in seeing your reality reflected in mainstream culture.

I still get a jolt of excitement when I see a family that looks like mine in an advert. I can't help it. Two little brown kids sitting having breakfast, or playing in the park, or building sandcastles, one white parent, one Black parent looking on. 'They look like us,' I think, and I smile. That could be my dad struggling to put up the Christmas lights, or my mum rubbing sun cream onto sandy, brown arms. It may seem like a tiny thing, but it legitimises our presence and tells the world that my family is what a British family can look like. It harks back to that quest for belonging. But underneath that heart-squeezing feeling of recognition is something else – a nagging suspicion.

I have a sense that we – mixed families – are being used and rendered voiceless in the process. We are literally being objectified to sell products, but what do these adverts actually add to the public's understanding of what it means to be mixed? Is it anything beyond the superficial? I worry about the longer-term implications of this sudden, intense focus on an incredibly narrow cross-section of mixed models. The intense backlash that big brands face every single year for featuring mixed families in their campaigns – the accusations of a 'woke' agenda – also suggests that this kind of messaging isn't doing anything to actually improve acceptance or reduce racism.

_____

7   Lloyds Banking Group, Diversity Report, 2016

Beyond the representations of interracial families, mixed models and actresses are increasingly being centred in advertising campaigns, helping to keep brands up to date with the latest standards of aspirational beauty, and win some 'diversity' points in the process. These models aren't voiceless or blind, however, many of them know exactly what's happening. It's an incredibly fine and complicated line that sits somewhere between opportunity and exploitation.

Laura is an actress and a model. Her dad is Nigerian and Portuguese, her mum is Nigerian and English and Laura spent much of her childhood living in Nigeria. Her race and racialised physical features has had a direct impact on the kind of work she can get in the industry, and how much money she can make. It shifts depending on moving cultural trends and even on something as seemingly superficial as how she chooses to wear her hair.

'Ever since I made the decision to leave my hair natural and stop straightening it, I have not been cast in a single corporate job. Not one,' said Laura. Her hair is tightly coiled and bounces just above her shoulders. She wears it with an off-centre parting, and it springs about her face as she talks.

Laura is convinced that her hair is the cause of this drastic decline in paid opportunities. Corporate jobs were a lifeline for Laura, a way for her to pursue more creative channels. Without them, she's a bit stuck.

'It's directly related to my hair, I look too African, I look too Black – which I didn't when I had my hair straight,' she told me. She added that casting directors don't think that she looks like she belongs in an office when she has her natural hair out.

'Even when I go for my auditions with my hair up or tied in a neat bun – it doesn't matter. 'It's like: if my hair isn't straight and I'm not emulating European beauty standards then I just don't get a look in. It's insane.'

Laura told me that for mainstream commercials – for streetwear and sports brands – she can almost always get in the room, but for corporate jobs she can't even get an audition. She is living proof that the advertising boom that favours mixed faces is still an incredibly exclusive and superficial world. What she has experienced reinforces the idea that it's not that advertisers have any interest in genuinely diverse representation; they are looking for an incredibly specific, sellable look.

'I don't have the "right type" of mixed-race hair,' explained Laura, tugging fondly at one of her coils. She let it go and it sprung right back up towards her ear. I remember similar reactions when I first started embracing my own natural hair. I was called 'urban' by a colleague; another friend expressed their shock at the size and volume of my hair. I was definitely treated as more of an 'other' with my natural coils, or when my hair was in braids. For Laura, this shift in how she was perceived has impacted her livelihood.

'My hair is not long. Shrinkage is real, the curls are tight and it has definitely been affected because I have been straightening it for so long. My hair stops growing at a certain point. It's not the "perfect" mixed Afro; it's not the long, loose curls you see in adverts.'

With her straight hair, Laura made it to the final round of auditions for an Emirates commercial in which she believed they had been looking for Asian women. With her hair straight Laura tells me that she can look like she could be from anywhere, and directors eat that up.

'That seems to be what works in the world of advertising. Ambiguity. The moment my Blackness starts to show through too strongly – that doesn't work for them.

'You see it over and over again in casting calls; they are looking for mixed-race women, and they are completely open about that. It's just yet another thing that I think perpetuates the colourism narrative. And that is exactly what they want – to create division even within Black communities, and lots of mixed-race people are part of Black communities. By constantly pushing mixed-race women into the spotlight and leaving out darker-skinned women and Black women, people with power are just reinforcing these divisions and pitting us against each other.'

By focusing on this select group of mixed models and families, while continuing to exclude Black, Asian or any other monoracial minorities, advertisers and brands are showing their hand. What they are actually after is ambiguity, not diversity. The aim is not to truly represent the different communities that make up Britain today, the aim is simply to make money off the aesthetics of racial fluidity.

Trends in beauty standards come in waves before disappearing into the ether. That's fine when those standards revolve around a certain haircut or make-up style, but when the 'trend' is a racialised feature, it becomes incredibly problematic. What happens when it's no longer cool to look like us?

The celebration of ethnically ambiguous features by celebrity culture has propagated and accelerated the myth of mixed beauty. The Kardashians are the perfect example of this. They have created a racial identity that appears consciously obscure, picking up the features of Blackness that work to their advantage – from their skin tone to their body types and their hair styles – and seemingly ignoring the elements that don't, like living with the daily realities of systemic racism. The tricky thing is when being mixed is conflated with this Kardashian-esque selectiveness, as though any of us had any say in the texture of our hair, the colour of eyes or our skin tone. This is the kind of thinking that leads to the fetishisation of mixed babies and children.

My boyfriend and I are now at the age where we are being asked about children, relentlessly. The fascination with the appearance of these theoretical, future kids is unsettling. 'They're going to be *so* beautiful,' people gush. 'Imagine if they have Jared's eyes with your skin!' or, 'They'll be such a gorgeous colour.' As flattering as it is to be repeatedly told that my children are going to be stunning, it's weird that everyone's first thoughts are about how they are going to look. I don't think couples of the same ethnic background are subject to this kind of forensic dissection of their as yet non-existent offspring.

The comments are well-meaning, for the most part, but it makes me feel like my relationship, my family, my possible future babies, are a spectacle, fair game for analysis and judgement. It stresses me out to think that if I do ever have a child, the first thing people will do is hold up a colour chart in their mind and try to fit this kid somewhere on that spectrum. What will be the implications of that kind of judgement for my child? What if they don't happen to be 'blessed' with the 'best' parts of my Blackness?

For now, most of society appears to be accepting, embracing, even covetous of mixed people in terms of ideas about how we look. The reasoning behind this acceptance is at least partly problematic, as discussed above, but that doesn't change facts. Right now, we are the 'in' thing. But it wasn't always like this. It wasn't always cool to be mixed. Only a few decades back, being mixed was a pitiable condition. There was the assumption that we were rootless, adrift without meaningful familial or ancestral ties, that there was something deviant about

our 'cross-breeding' parents, that we represented a contamina-
tion of 'racial purity'. It harks back to the post-slavery 'tragic
mulatto' trope, which saw mixed men and women painted
as wretched creatures, cast aside by all, accepted by no one.

It wasn't all that long ago that mixed people – regardless
of what we looked like – were thought of as the lowest of
the low; genetically undesirable, stupid, contaminated, tragic.
In the 1930s there were groups releasing warnings about the
dangers of what they called 'race-crossing'. The dominance of
eugenics during this period was particularly impactful on how
the mixed population of Britain was viewed. Marie Stopes,
who was a prominent race scientist at the time, advocated
that all 'half castes' should be 'sterilised at birth'. Earlier than
this, after World War Two, the Foreign Office forcibly split
up interracial families in an attempt to prevent more mixed
children from being born; 1,362 Chinese sailors who had
settled in Liverpool after serving in the Merchant Navy were
forcibly repatriated after the war, despite the fact that at least
150 were married to British women and had up to 450 children
between them.[8] In Britain, within the space of 100 years, we
have gone from public calls to surgically prevent the mixed
population from procreating, to being held up as the model
of modern beauty.[9]

Even growing up in the 1990s, there was none of the
widespread reverence of mixed people that we see today. The
brazen hostility of the 1970s and 1980s had shifted and faded,
but my mother was still stared at – glared at – for leaving the
house with two brown babies in tow. People made assumptions

8   Laura Smith, 'Mixed Race Britain: Charting the Social History', Guard-
ian, 4th October, 2011
9   Hall, R, 'Marie Stopes: A Biography', Andre Deutsch Limited London,
1977

about her for her decision to love a Black man, and they openly assumed that my dad wasn't around based purely on the fact that he was a Black man. Despite our current trendiness and the superficial acceptance we now see in the media, many of these disapproving and hostile attitudes still persist today.

On ITV's reality television show *Love Island*, on two separate occasions in 2018, two of the white, female contestants said that they were particularly attracted to mixed men. One of the women simply said, 'I do love mixed race.' Neither of them apparently saw any issue with making these statements, and nobody on the show called them out for it (although there was some backlash to the remarks on Twitter and an article or two). Frequently, statements like these by white women are followed up with an admission of a desire for mixed babies, as though it is somehow possible to engineer the perfect cocktail of racialised features and the ideal level of exoticism for their offspring. The hostility that mixed individuals once faced has morphed into something different, something more insidious and subtle, but equally problematic.

Western society's collective obsession with brown babies is, quite frankly, creepy. There are whole Facebook groups and Twitter accounts dedicated to mixed kids. 'Swirl' YouTube channels hosted by interracial couples and their children rack up thousands of views. The hashtag #MixedBabies has 1.7 million posts on Instagram, and the comments under these pictures invariably focus on how 'beautiful' the child is, the texture of their hair, the colour of their eyes, their 'caramel' skin tone.

The sexualisation and obsession with looks starts at a disturbingly young age and follows mixed people well into adulthood. But only if you're the 'right' kind of mixed. Where we happen to fall on this beauty scale is completely dependent on our specific racial heritage, age, gender and a whole host of other contextual factors. But the over-representation of one kind of mixed appearance in mainstream media gives the impression that all mixed people are viewed like this, which just isn't the case at all.

On the surface, it may seem like a positive thing to be told that we're beautiful, but the unspoken othering that exists alongside these declarations make it anything but. Today we are exoticised as beautiful, sixty years ago we were painted as repulsive, but the message is the same however you dress it up: we're different. And no matter how much people say that being lauded for your beauty is a compliment, the hyper-focus on the aesthetic appearance of mixed people feels more reductive and insulting than anything remotely positive.

Alexander, who I spoke to in Chapter 3, knows the specific experience of being exoticised as a gay man. He says being approached in this way feels like objectification of the worst kind; racial fetishisation framed as a compliment.

'I get people using my skin colour as a pick-up line. A lot. It speaks of a certain ignorance, and definitely of fetishisation. I get the word "exotic" as well. I really hate the word exotic used as a compliment because it's not a compliment. Essentially it means different. Different but nice . . . but still different.'

One example that sticks in Alexander's mind happened during his first experience of a gay club in London. It was an incident that he thinks epitomises the way mixed people are often reduced to how they aesthetically present to the world, and little more.

'I was dancing, I'd had a couple of drinks, and this white British guy came up to me and asked me if I was Maori,' said Alexander. He's animated as he talks and has a lyrical Aussie lilt.

'I said, "Er, no, I'm not," and he looked actually sad and put out when I told him I wasn't. He said, "Oh, Maoris are my favourite." He was genuinely disappointed. It was so weird.

'I told him my dad is Sri Lankan, but he just kept pushing it: "But you sound like you're Maori?" I explained that no, that's just because I grew up in Australia. And he literally just turned around and walked away from me without another word.'

Alexander finished his tale with a sad smile; I could tell how hurtful that was for him, particularly as one of his formative interactions in London's gay scene. It was a rejection based on him not meeting the specific requirements of somebody else's racial fetish, which was a lot to unpack.

Racial fetishisation is a sexual version of racial stereotyping. It is where certain features or qualities attributed to a specific racial group are hypersexualised, fantasised about, lusted after. The 'fieriness' of Latina women, the 'promiscuity' of Black women, the 'subservience' of Asian women, the 'exoticness' of mixed women – these are just a handful of the ways racial groups are fetishised using archaic stereotypes.

I mention women because that's my direct experience with being fetishised, but as Alexander proves, it happens to men too. In his incredible book about race and class in the UK, *Natives*, author and academic Akala highlighted the treatment of British athlete Linford Christie by the press after he won gold in the 100m at the 1992 Olympics.

'In the days and weeks after Linford's historic victory, the press was not focused on his contribution to British sport, but instead full of stories about "Linford's lunchbox", a less than subtle euphemism for his apparently huge penis,'[10] Akala wrote.

---

10 Akala, 'Natives: Race and Class in the Ruins of Empire', Two Roads, John Murray Press, 2018

It was an image that would endure, with the *Daily Star* referencing the sprinter's allegedly generous endowment in a headline as recently as 2016, when Linford appeared on a reality TV show where celebrities attempt to learn how to ski jump: 'Lunchbox Linford keeps massive ski pole hidden for photoshoot', read the header, with the article continuing, 'He carefully positioned his skis over his famous crown jewels which have been dubbed Linford's Lunchbox.'

The man won gold for this country in arguably the most prestigious event at the Olympics and yet, twenty-four years later, the press is still obsessing over what's in his pants. The Linford Christie debacle was before my time, but this widespread obsession with the size and voracity of Black male genitalia has never gone away. Gravitating towards Black guys on the assumption that they have large penises is a fetish. It's a projection of a demeaning sexual stereotype and it even feeds into archaic tropes that associate Black men with sexual violence.

Men of colour can be fetishised in other less obvious ways as well. Think about how Chancellor (at the time of writing) Rishi Sunak was presented after delivering one or two comparatively coherent press conferences during the coronavirus lockdown. He was almost instantly dubbed 'Dishy Rishi' and white women repeatedly declared their 'surprise' at fancying him on Twitter; a couple of white journalists even wrote think pieces dissecting their 'unexpected' attraction to Rishi, calling it a 'dirty little secret'.

For some, of course, the dirty secret here is that they fancy a Tory politician, and their discomfort stems from a conflict of politics, but there is also a sense that some of these writers are betraying an internalised shame and obvious bewilderment at finding themselves even vaguely attracted to an Asian man, which may be a consequence of the stereotypes of desexualisation historically attached to this group. How could these white women possibly comprehend an attraction to an Asian man when they are unrelentingly presented in the media and in mainstream Western culture as non-sexual, nerdy, unattractive?

A writer analysing the chancellor's 'baffling' attractiveness in a UK *Vogue* article said, 'Swotty Sunak reminds you of the medic you had a crush on in the first term of your first year: smart, focused and earnest, bright eyes twinkling with sincerity.'[11] There it is. 'Swotty', 'medical student', 'focused'; the stereotypes of the studious, obedient minority aren't even remotely subtle.

Obviously, being fetishised is not a compliment. It's a reduction of who you are to a litany of sexual parts, it's a racist and often misogynistic objectification that highlights an intensely unsettling relationship between desirability and racial hierarchies. It can never be a compliment because there is always a power dynamic at play. The fetishiser holds more power than the fetishised (a white man can fetishise an Asian woman, or a Black woman, a white woman can fetishise a Black man – but it doesn't work the other way around) and holding that power over somebody else is often part of the attraction.

A fetish is a projection of the fetishiser's own fantasies, which strips the fetishised of all individuality, all autonomy, and offers them up as the severed components of an idea. Somebody saying that they 'love mixed-race girls' is really not the compliment they might think it is – it's a violence.

'When I was growing up, I experienced a lot of fetishisation, but I never really coded that as racism,' Alexander explained. 'I always thought it was kind of a *nice* thing that

---

11 Phoebe Luckhurst, 'Admit it: You fancy Rishi Sunak', Vogue UK, April 2020

people were bestowing on me. They would say, "Oh you're so exotic and you're so special and you're so beautiful," and I just thought, oh, I guess I am. Obviously, you internalise that as a nice thing.'

It wasn't until adulthood that Alexander began to realise that fetishisation is really a form of discrimination. 'It's basically reducing the complexity of who I am down to the attributes that that person thinks are important – in this case, the aesthetic. I think that's a really tricky space to fill, when you're living that,' he said.

'Being told that you're attractive always feels lovely, of course, but then you realise where it comes from. You realise that the person complimenting you – and it's always a white person – has decided to prioritise that part of who you are, above and beyond anything else. You start to realise that these compliments come from more of a nefarious source, which is essentially racism.'

Alexander knows that this isn't the most pernicious or damaging form of racism by any stretch of the imagination, but he also thinks that these experiences shouldn't be dismissed outright just because they seem positive on the surface. He wants to push back against this kind of fetishisation, and in order to do that, it's important to be able to acknowledge that it does have detrimental effects.

'Darker-skinned Black and brown people are much more likely to experience racism that is more hurtful and more likely to put their safety at risk, so we can't compare our experiences. At the same time, it's also important for people to acknowledge fetishisation as a very particular, subtle and insidious form of racial discrimination. And I think it should be identified as such, because otherwise, our experience of that as mixed-race people is denied if we don't call it what it is.'

The kind of fetishisation that Alexander is describing is specific to mixed people who are part white because it is entirely dependent on that proximity to whiteness. And that's why making sweeping statements about the collective hotness of mixed people isn't a compliment – it's nothing more than a reinforcement of a racial hierarchy that still positions whiteness above everything else.

Studies have found that there are high levels of sexual racism in the gay dating scene, or at least more brazen and unapologetic discrimination. An Australian study in 2015 found that 96 per cent of Grindr users had viewed at least one profile that included some sort of racial discrimination, and more than half reported that they had been victims of racism while using the app[12]. Researchers concluded that sexual racism 'is closely associated with generic racist attitudes, which challenges the idea of racial attraction as solely a matter of personal preference'. A 2019 US study confirmed that racism on queer dating apps can have significant negative health impacts on men of colour – including causing depression.[13] Most research on the health of young gay men of colour has focused on HIV and sexual health, but the authors of this study said there is a demonstrable need for research examining racism and psychosocial functioning among this population. 'Sexual racism is an important but under-investigated phenomenon that may have implications for the psychological health and

---

12 Denton Callander, Christie E. Newman, Martin Holt, 'Is Sexual Racism Really Racism? Distinguishing Attitudes Toward Sexual Racism and Generic Racism Among Gay and Bisexual Men', Archives of Sexual Behaviour, Vol. 44, Issue 7, July 2015
13 Ryan Wade and Gary Harper, 'Racialized Sexual Discrimination (RSD) in the Age of Online Sexual Networking: Are Young Black Gay/Bisexual Men (YBGBM) at Elevated Risk for Adverse Psychological Health?', American Journal of Community Psychology, Vol. 65, October 2019

well-being of young Black gay/bisexual men,' reads the study abstract.

'So, an app like Grindr is essentially a hook-up app; we tell ourselves it's a dating app, but it's a hook-up app,' Alexander told me. 'It has commodified sex, intimacy and romance to the point where you can filter your exact specifications. We all fill out our height, weight, preferred sexual position and ethnicity as part of our profiles, which are variables that you don't include on an app like Tinder.'

Alexander thinks the layout and the functioning of these apps allows for more exclusion and sexual racism – it gives people the tools to act in a discriminatory way much easier. You can choose not to disclose your ethnicity on these apps, but enough people are using it to filter their results for it to become a problem.

'It's instantly problematic, right? It allows white people to literally just filter out anyone who isn't white. Or you can only speak to mixed people if that's your fetish. I don't think the gay community is any more racist than the straight community, I just think we have the tools that make it easier to act in this way.'

Since I first spoke to Alexander, Grindr has actually removed this function. It's no longer possible to filter your matches based on ethnicity. But, while the move has been applauded as a positive step towards weeding out racism on the app, some have raised concerns that the ethnicity filter was actually a helpful tool for queer men of colour. Some say the tool helped them to actively avoid those with racist views and matches that could lead to harmful interactions. The mixed response suggests that removing the filter probably isn't the quick fix for tackling racism that developers hoped it would be.

Racial fetishisation certainly isn't something that is confined to the gay dating scene. Heterosexual mixed people deal with these problematic interactions on dating apps all the time: 'compliments' focused entirely on certain racialised features, othering framed as sexual desire, being told you're somebody's 'type' simply because you're not white but not *too* Black, either. It can be a minefield trying to differentiate between fetishisation and genuine, authentic attraction.

My sister Becky has been online dating since before it was a thing that everyone did. When she first started, maybe ten years ago, people were more upfront about their racial 'preferences'. She would frequently see white guys spelling it out in the bios of their profile pages. *'Loves Black girls and mixed-race girls.'* She says it's harder to weed out the guys who think like this now. People tend to be less open about it, but Becky says it's definitely still there – the language around it has just become more coded.

'Out of nowhere, this guy who I had only just started talking to said: "I bet you're like an animal in bed,"' Becky told me. '"Animal" didn't sit right with me at all, and then he said mixed-race girls are just "different" in bed. What does that even mean?'

It makes complete sense for Becky to be offended by this clear example of racial fetishisation. This guy was linking her racial 'otherness', as he saw it, with an assumption that it would somehow make her better, dirtier and less inhibited in the bedroom. He wasn't even remotely ashamed to voice these thoughts and didn't see anything wrong with them.

Becky says she often gets the sense that men are excited by the fact they see her as 'other', as though that otherness is going to provide some unique, game-changing sexual experience for them. They also seem excited to tell her that they have never slept with a mixed or Black girl before, as though she's going to be honoured at having the opportunity to pop their ethnic cherry.

'Guys also say to me a lot – you're just so "sexy". Who even uses the word "sexy"? No one under the age of 40 surely,' she laughed. 'I really doubt they would use that word talking to a white girl.

'It comes under the same category as "spicy", "exotic", "Amazonian"; these are all words men have used to describe me on Tinder in the last six months. I hate it. It suggests that they don't see me as a person, they just see a collection of features. It's irrelevant what I'm like, or how funny I am, or what I talk about, because regardless of whether they actually find *me* that attractive, they have decided that they are attracted to the concept of me, to the *idea* of me.'

Fetishising or exoticising mixed people is never a compliment, no matter how it's dressed up; whether it's sexual fetishising in the world of dating, the boom of ethnically ambiguous features in ad campaigns and on social media, or well-meaning friends obsessing about how your future children might look or expressing their own hopes for a mixed baby. This kind of treatment is reductive, divisive, and only serves to turn mixed people into commodities with a value that is dependent on dilution, on partial whiteness.

At the same time, this narrative actively excludes mixed people who don't have a white parent, those who don't necessarily have lighter skin or any of that all-important palatability, which is what so much of this kind of fetishisation is dependent on. If you're mixed without white heritage – a so-called 'minority mix' – it may protect you to some extent from this specific kind of racial fetishisation, but there are many other complex issues to consider. This group is frequently ignored in conversations about mixedness, and too often whiteness is centred in these discussions. But it is vital to remember that there is more than one way to be mixed.

# Chapter 5

# The 'Right Type of Mixed' and 'Minority Mixes'

In May 2018, Prince Harry married Meghan Markle and the wedding day was an explosion of overblown British traditionalism on an epic scale. I was actually there on the big day, in Windsor. No, not as a guest, nor as a Union Jack-waving enthusiast with Pimms and a picnic basket (I'm not a closet Royalist) – I was there for work. The BBC asked me to talk about the significance of the day on 5Live, so they hauled me out of bed at 5 a.m. and paid for me to take a taxi all the way from North London for a series of live chats throughout the build-up and aftermath of the Royal nuptials. It would be my first experience of live radio, and I was pretty nervous.

It made sense to invite me. I had written an article for *gal-dem* about Meghan and how the wedding didn't herald any great step forward for race relations in the UK. I had also recorded a number of interviews about the couple on the radio in the months preceding. And, of course, I was mixed – the right kind of mixed. Meghan-mixed. And in the eyes of the BBC, it seems that this in itself gave me an inherent authority to speak on these matters, to become their 'mixed-race spokesperson' for the day.

It was going to be warm, but when I arrived in Windsor at 7 a.m., the blue chill of a spring dawn still clung to the air and I wrapped my oversized jacket tightly around my flimsy spaghetti-strapped slip dress. I'm not entirely sure why I dressed up to go on the radio, but it felt right at the time. It was a wedding, after all.

Goosebumps sprang up on my bare legs and I ducked into McDonald's for a cup of tea – more to warm my hands than anything else – before heading towards the media trucks. The trucks, trailers and gazebos of the world's press were stationed in silent, gleaming anticipation all along the grand driveway where the couple would take their first carriage ride as newlyweds later that day. Harassed-looking producers darted between them carrying clipboards and barking into headsets.

I found my production team and they sat me on a plastic chair at the flapping entrance to a tent where I was to wait for my first stint on air. I positioned my chilly legs in the sun and scrolled Twitter as the day warmed slowly around me and throngs of people began to pack into the green spaces and cluster around the giant screens, hoping to catch a glimpse of the couple arriving, or at least some of the celebrity guests.

The streets of Windsor had been cleared of homeless people for the occasion, bunting danced from lamp-post to lamp-post, pastel-coloured balloons strained for the sky at the doorways of cafés and trinket shops. It was a spotless veneer of quintessential Britishness. Apart from one, unavoidable thing.

'What does it mean to have a mixed-race member of the Royal Family?' the presenter asked me as we went live for the first time that morning. I had my spiel prepared. It didn't mean a thing. This wasn't the progressive symbol of unity and hope that many media pundits were trying to sell. It wasn't an indication that we were moving into some kind of 'post-racial' utopia where people of all ethnic backgrounds were granted equal opportunities – far from it. And sadly, this was an argument I was to be proven correct on as Meghan would be hounded out of the Royal Family, out of the country even, just two years later by the virulent, relentless and disproportionate criticism and abuse at the hands of the British press and commentators on every platform. But we didn't know that then, and the BBC was, it seemed, determined to see Meghan's official inauguration into Britain's most elitist establishment as something more than surface tokenism.

The presenter couldn't win me round, and I watched him choke down an incredulous laugh as I said that I didn't care what Royalists thought of Meghan, and he winced as I called the Royal Family an 'increasingly archaic and irrelevant institution' live on air. I don't think it was exactly the irreverent tone the producers had been hoping for when they booked their contributors for the day. Shortly after this comment, I spotted a message on the host's iPad from one of his producers that read something along the lines of: 'If you go back to her – keep it light.' I had to laugh. The next time they threw to my host, he asked me about David Beckham arriving and my predictions for Meghan's dress – not quite my areas of expertise.

When I wasn't giving producers heart attacks by refusing to stick to their script, most of the day was spent waiting around. As I killed some time wandering among the tartan picnic blankets and fluttering Union Jacks, soaking up the sun and marvelling at the eccentricities of the crowds, I reflected on that question for myself. What *did* it mean to have a mixed Royal with Black heritage in the UK? There were a lot of Black and mixed people in the crowds, and it clearly meant something to them. But I couldn't shake the feeling that Meghan was only being allowed into this space because she fitted a very specific blueprint of mixedness, and that any deviation of her heritage, how she looked or presented herself would have caused the door to slam in her face (even faster than it actually did).

One thing that really stuck out from those early days of Meghan-mania – before the nasty campaign against her properly set in – was the fact that she was presented as the 'right' kind of mixed. In fact, the *only* kind of mixed. As every publication wrote articles and produced programmes about being mixed, specifically tied to Meghan, she became synonymous with the mixed experience. By mainstream understanding, to be mixed was to be like Meghan – a combination of Black and white that translates tidily onto your physical features. As I also fit this blueprint of widely accepted mixedness, I had never had to think about it before. But, as Meghan's face was plastered over countless feature articles, and people who looked exactly like me were given platforms to analyse and comment on mixedness, it became clear just how narrow this perspective is.

My mix – Black Caribbean and white British – is the most commonly recorded mixed ethnicity in the UK. And as a result, the endless other ways in which people can be mixed are frequently erased from the conversation entirely. And the prevalence of this kind of mix isn't the only reason why it dominates discussions, it's also because it includes whiteness.

Underpinning most discussions about mixedness is the assumption that whiteness features somewhere in the equation. Whiteness is the baseline, the default, and anything that comes on top of that is an interesting, 'exotic' talking point. If you're mixed with two non-white ethnicities, society loses interest. Anything beyond this binary is categorised as 'other' and the intricacies and nuances of your heritage are not deemed worthy of wider discussion, or even clear categorisation.

Just take a look at the mixed options on the census and ethnicity forms. There are three distinct categories for mixed individuals to tick: white and Black Caribbean, white and Black African, white and Asian. The fact that 'white' always comes first in these descriptions is likely because the UK is still a majority-white country, but it feels like another nod to the fact that whiteness is always seen as the norm from which all other categories deviate.

Then, at the bottom, there is a fourth category: 'other mixed'. This is the singular option for the myriad ethnicity potentials within the mixed experience that don't include whiteness. They all have to share one vaguer than vague box. On many forms, there isn't even the space to expand your answer and record your specific heritage. If you don't fit those first three boxes of 'white-plus-something', then you're effectively discounted. It sends a message that so-called 'minority mix' ethnicities hold less value than mixes that include whiteness.

Of course this would be the attitude in a society that is built on a racial hierarchy with a snowy peak of whiteness at the top. The closer you are to whiteness, the more valued you are, which is why so many of the conversations about mixedness are about privilege, proximity to whiteness, distance from whiteness and passing as white. It's why there are so few academic studies, books and essays about the experiences of people with multiple minority heritage. It's like we are only able to discuss ethnicity in terms of whiteness, and without that central pin, everyone else is ignored and erased from the blueprint altogether.

On the wedding day in Windsor, I thought about Meghan and how she had come to be standing on those church steps in her white silk dress, veil twisting in the wind, news cameras from around the globe following her every step towards the enormous arched door, towards her new life.

Meghan's mother Doria, her only attending family member, looked incongruous with her dark skin and carefully styled dreadlocks, against a sea of powdered pallid faces in the pews around her. Would Meghan have been allowed to enter this space if she didn't have white heritage, if she didn't have an aesthetic proximity to whiteness that reflected in the lightness of her skin and the glossy sheen of her straightened hair? I suspect not. So, when we talk about mixedness, about the privileges and the strangeness of existing in liminal space, usually the space we are referring to is between whiteness and something else. But it's vital to remember that people exist in so many other liminal spaces too, spaces far removed from whiteness.

This is one of the key reasons why we can't homogenise the mixed experience. Despite the clear common threads that tie our experiences together, the difference in value according to our heritage ensures that we experience the world differently, so we can never be lumped together as one. Those who are mixed without whiteness are perceived as 'other', treated as 'other', excluded from conversations of mixedness and exist without the privileges that come with proximity to whiteness. By ignoring their stories, we are propping up the hierarchical constructions of race and reinforcing the idea that whiteness has more value than everything else.

As the newlywed Royal couple left the church for their carriage procession through the immaculate streets of Windsor, a ripple swept the crowds, and everyone began to edge towards the barriers alongside the driveway where the carriage would pass. This is what they had come here for – a glimpse of royalty, the sensation of being physically close to power, of existing in the same space as the elite. I rolled my eyes at the jostling crowd, but I didn't tear my gaze away from the driveway. The screams, whistles and claps rose and swelled as the carriage drew closer and people scrambled to their feet, knocked over jugs of Pimms and abandoned their picnic blankets to get closer.

I didn't move, but as the couple rolled into my eyeline, their gilded carriage dazzling in the sun, I was surprised to feel a thrill of giddiness. Given I had spent the morning telling the entire nation how ludicrous and outdated I find the concept of the monarchy, I didn't expect to feel any kind of way when the Royal newlyweds passed by. But when I actually saw Meghan beaming next to her new husband just a few feet away — a woman who looks like me being presented to the world as a symbol of ultimate Britishness — as foolish as it sounds, I couldn't help but feel a pang of hope. I felt my arm shoot up above my head, as though it had a mind of its own, and I waved frantically at Meghan as she passed.

The events of the following two years would prove that this giddy moment of optimism was misplaced. Meghan was never going to be an acceptable symbol; her presence alone was never going to improve this country's attitude towards minorities. No matter how close to whiteness she was, she would never be white enough. But the fact that I felt that hope simply at seeing her roll by in that carriage, the fact that I felt compelled to wave at her like an idiot and try to catch her eye, shows that visual representation can have an impact. Even if representation alone can never be enough to create lasting change, I do believe it is important in fostering a sense of belonging, a sense of acknowledgement that you are seen, that you exist.

As we discussed in Chapter 4, Exoticisation, Fetishisation and Othering, in recent years, visual representation of mixedness has boomed. But this representation only extends to people who are the 'right' kind of mixed; those of us who are mixed in a way deemed acceptable and covetable by society – those of us who are Meghan-mixed, mixed with whiteness.

If we don't find a way to decentre whiteness when talking about mixed experiences and identity, we will never create a full, realistic picture of what it means to be mixed, and the many varied intricacies. And by repeatedly talking about mixed ethnicity only in terms of whiteness, we are simply bolstering the idea that whiteness is the starting point on which everything else depends. Dismantling this system begins with creating space for other narratives and alternative blueprints.

Bilal has a mixed background without white heritage. His dad is Kenyan, but Asian Kenyan as Bilal's grandparents were Kashmiri, then they moved to Kenya. Bilal's mum is from Jamaica, but she's also mixed – her dad's origins are from somewhere in South Asia – and her mum, Bilal's maternal grandmother, is Black Caribbean.

That's quite a lot to explain if Bilal is ever asked, 'Where are you *really* from?' And this question comes up a lot. His answers vary depending on who's asking and what mood he happens to be in.

'If it's someone I'm interested in talking to, then I'll tell them the whole story. But if it's not, they might get a condensed version, or nothing at all,' Bilal told me.

We sat facing each other on two of the squashy leather sofas in my office atrium on a freezing afternoon. I felt a rush of gratitude to be considered one of the people Bilal was interested in talking to.

Bilal is hard to miss. He has enviably thick, dark hair that falls below his shoulders. When we spoke, he had swept it up in a glossy knot on top of his head and I had to resist the urge to ask him for his wash-day tips. He dressed in block-colours – a nineties-style oversized jacket over dungarees and a bold T-shirt, a gold ring in his nose. He gave off the kind of comfortable eccentricity unique to people who grew up in London, exposed to the unapologetic individualism of the city.

'The other day we went to Spoons, me and a couple of mates,' he told me (we were speaking prior to the Covid-19 pandemic). 'We were outside having a cigarette and this guy comes up to me and he's like – "Where are you from?" – just out of nowhere.

'My mates burst out laughing; they knew he had chosen the wrong person to ask that question. I thought, "We're not going to have this conversation," so I just shut it down. That's always how I react when I don't want to talk about that stuff. People act like they are entitled to my full family back story, just by looking at me.'

Bilal agrees with me that ideas of mixedness are always centred on the assumption that you are white and 'something else'. But he, and thousands of others, are living proof that there is more than one way to be mixed. He told me he finds it frustrating that people like him rarely feature in mainstream conversations about mixedness. Bilal believes we can get so much more understanding and insight about mixed identity when we consider these different perspectives and push back against the dominant pull of whiteness.

'Being mixed without that proximity to whiteness opens up a whole range of new ideas. When we discuss what being mixed-race means, the elements that come up again and again are usually to do with whiteness; conversations about dealing with racist members of your white family, for example. As a result, the story of mixedness becomes focused on the nega-tive and challenging aspects. People get really caught up in the idea that being mixed is *always* hard, is *always* confusing, because of the fraught relationship between whiteness and any other race.

'But that isn't the same for other ethnic groups. I think if you start talking about people who are mixed with minoritised ethnic backgrounds, it just gets more interesting. You start to have conversations that don't usually get heard.'

One of these key conversations often missing is about the relationship between South Asian and Black people – like the relationship between Bilal's parents. He said these are fascinating, multi-layered relationships that are rarely looked at, and talking about this neglected dynamic opens up a whole new way to understand being mixed.

'It's so important to think about what it means when *other* cultures come together, not just how they interact with white culture,' he added.

I found myself nodding vigorously during my entire conversation with Bilal. He has a knack for explaining complex, nuanced ideas with a simplicity and clarity that makes it impossible not to engage, which isn't surprising given that his profession is delivering training on diversity and inclusion – a job which, in his words, involves a lot of standing in rooms full of white people and telling them about themselves.

One concept that Bilal laid out incredibly clearly was the problematic nature of the relationship between whiteness and every other race; relationships that are so often characterised by opposition, hierarchy, superiority and difference. But relationships between other races – although often impacted by notions of white supremacy – tend to be much more positive, unified and collaborative. This is something Bilal has seen within his own family and in the many commonalities between his Asian and Caribbean heritage.

'Recently, my mum and dad went to Kenya for the first time, together,' Bilal told me. 'My dad had never been back since he moved to this country in 1973, so it was a whole world away for him. I guess he had never gone back because he got scared of what home was going to be like. We've been to Jamaica six or seven times as a family, so we have seen where my mum's from. And I've seen Kenya before – I've been there on my own. I saw that Kenya and Jamaica share so much in common, but my parents had never seen that first-hand.

'I think it brought them closer together because they finally saw these commonalities between their two cultures. There were similarities in the types of rural countryside, the way that people are with each other – in terms of sharing things and politeness – the mannerisms and behaviours were similar to some degree. Obviously, there are differences between Asian culture and Caribbean culture and traditions, but there are so many things that tied them together.'

Of course, removing whiteness from the equation isn't a guarantee of racial harmony, and there are conflicts, difficulties and prejudices across many different racial divides. There is a well-recorded problem of anti-Blackness in South Asian communities.

In an article about this specific form of racial prejudice, academic Dr Fatima Rajina explained that there isn't enough support for Black lives among South Asians and highlighted the need for people in these communities to unlearn some damaging biases.

'The [South Asian] community holds onto well-established tropes about the Black community, including the belief that they bring their suffering upon themselves[1],' said Dr Rajina.

---

1  Faima Bakar, 'The South Asian guide to supporting Black people in a more sustainable way', Metro.co.uk, 3rd June, 2020

'This is dismissive and completely denies the way this society is organised in a way that enables the mistreatment of Black communities. South Asian communities take comfort, basically, in knowing they are not Black, implicitly accepting their proximity to whiteness and that they will remain untouched.'

The anti-Blackness can manifest as prejudice, discriminatory treatment, violence and the erasure of Black Muslims. Within minority mixed families like Bilal's, these negative beliefs about Black people have caused deep animosities and conflicts in the past. Bilal says his dad's family took some convincing when he – Bilal's dad – first started dating a Black woman.

'My mum's family is interesting because they are Black and Asian mixed anyway, so when it came to my parents getting together, there was nothing to oppose or to find shocking because that had already happened. Whereas in my dad's family, they hadn't seen that before.

'My dad's parents, when they were alive, came from a culture of arranged marriages and doing things "traditionally", and a belief that everyone needs to be Muslim. My dad wasn't even particularly Muslim, and the family weren't really that religious themselves, but it was still a traditional culture.'

Bilal's dad started dating his mum when they were at school. When a relative found out what was going on, she snitched to the parents and told them their son was dating a Black girl, and his dad got in trouble. But it didn't break them up.

'No one said anything outright. No one said, "That's wrong", or "Don't do this". It was more a vibe that this is not what's done, I guess because it hadn't been done before.

'There was a lot of hostility in the early days. My parents were even considering becoming Muslim when I was born to try to appease the tension. But then, over the years, there was just this general acceptance. It took a bit of time, but everyone just got used to it, and then it was fine. My granddad – my dad's dad – passed away, and when he was dying, he wanted my mum around him all the time. By the time it got to that point, everyone was cool with everyone.'

Jeanette also grew up in London, but she has had a different experience to Bilal. Jeanette is Filipino and Cameroonian. She has luminous dark skin. Her hair is black, tightly coiled and springs up above her shoulders, framing her heart-shaped face and a smile full of big, white teeth. She told me that being mixed without whiteness has enhanced her ability to code-switch and has given her a different perspective on 'otherness'.

She also told me that, like Bilal, she has found being mixed with two minority heritages an incredibly welcoming experience. For Jeanette, there is something about being entirely outside of the spectrum of whiteness that feels both accepting and unified. She said there is a sense of solidarity that comes with having multiple, non-white identities.

'Otherness is inclusive, whereas whiteness is about the exclusion of everything else. It feels very oppositional, as though whiteness is this protected space that can't be entered, and that everyone else is on the other side. It feels very divisive and it really is this kind of exclusive club.

'That is not something I've ever felt from minority groups. I have always felt more unity and openness from people who aren't white; it's as though the differences aren't important – maybe because we are not seen as a threat to their power. I have always felt that minority spaces are welcoming and that they allow for diversity and difference.'

People are taken aback when Jeanette tells them she's mixed. She says there is still a very blinkered and limited expectation of what 'mixed' means, and with her dark skin tone and more typically Asian facial features, Jeanette doesn't fit that blueprint.

'When I was growing up, people only really saw me as Black. The landscape is different now and people are more likely to be aware that I might be mixed, but back then there was so little understanding. As a result, I always saw myself as "other" or Black, rather than mixed.

'I did feel on the outside of that mixedness club, and it used to bother me more when I was younger, for sure. When I was growing up, my best friend was mixed. She had a white mum and a Nigerian dad. I knew that she felt a kinship with me, but I also knew that other people didn't see us as part of the same group.

'No matter how much I might have wanted to put myself in that box, other people were always ready to take me out of it. Now, I identify as Black and mixed race, but it took me a long time to come to that, and that is, at least in part, because I didn't feel as though I belonged in that mixed space.'

But Jeanette did feel a longing to be part of that space. She felt as though mixed people were the only ones who would properly understand her experiences, who could relate to her on a different level.

'It would have been nice to have that connection, to feel as though I had an ally,' she explained. 'There are patterns and shared experiences that come with being mixed and I would have liked to have felt part of that. But at the same time, I know that things are changing, and my experience has changed. I feel like I grew up on the cusp of that conversation opening up, and I hope that if there were a young Jeanette now, she wouldn't feel on the outside.'

Jeanette is a similar age to me, and I can relate to this feeling. Growing up in the nineties and noughties, language around mixedness was still developing and coming into its own. Like Jeanette, I often wonder if it would be easier to be a teenager now? Would I have felt more accepted, more certain of who I was and where I fit? Speaking about mixedness with friends and colleagues as an adult, Jeanette has noticed that there is frequently a stark divide in opinions and attitudes between those mixed with white, and people who have mixed minority heritage.

'It's quite a different experience. From what I have heard and what I have read about being mixed, Black and white, they have one parent who has a lack of understanding of what it means to be "of colour",' she said. 'I'm not saying that having a parent of colour is the same as having a Black parent, it's not the same, but there is a connection there at least. When both of your parents are of colour, there are certain things that you don't have to explain.

'At the same time, there are things that my mum wouldn't necessarily see that I would see – because I'm Black, and she isn't. But the experience we have of the world is more similar than if I had a white parent because she is a person of colour. It did help with certain things when I was growing up. I didn't have to explain the nuances of racism, for example. I don't want this to sound like a mass generalisation because I'm not saying white people can't be "woke" about racism, but that isn't the same as having lived experiences.'

I think about coming home from primary school and telling my mum that a boy had called me 'chocolate face' in the playground, and that he was stealing things from my bag during PE and just generally making my life quite difficult. I can picture his face to this day. Telling my mum resulted in talks with the headteacher and the boy was punished, so I know she handled it, but I can't remember how Mum reacted when I initially brought it up. It must have been hard for her to confront – it was the first time I had told her about an experience of racism, and I didn't even know that it was racism. Would that have been easier for her – less shocking, or less foreign – if she was a person of colour, like Jeanette's mum?

Jeanette told me that she didn't feel comfortable identifying as 'mixed' for a long time because she says some people with mixed heritage use this label as a way of distancing themselves from their Blackness, which is something that she finds deeply problematic, and would never want to do.

'In my experience, it is more common for mixed people who are mixed with whiteness to identify themselves as mixed. A woman I used to work with, she's mixed: Black and white. If anyone referred her as Black, she would get annoyed and correct them, she would say – "Get it right – I'm mixed race."'

'While I can understand identifying as mixed, and there is nothing wrong with that, I find it odd when people with Black heritage actively want to differentiate and say that they are not Black. It's like they know that they will be rewarded for being different, and for distancing themselves from Blackness, which is why I think it is such an issue. And in my experience, that is an attitude more common in people who are mixed with whiteness, this desire for distance and clear divides between the two.

'So much of the benefits and privileges that come with being perceived as mixed are wrapped up in colonial thinking. You're praised because of your hair texture or your skin tone, you're praised for the attributes that mark you as not being purely Black – and that's a dangerous way to view yourself and others.'

Like me, Jeanette identifies as both mixed and Black. She wants her identity to recognise the specific experiences of having multiple heritage, without denying her Blackness. This is one small way Jeanette attempts to chip away at the embedded hierarchies that consistently position being Black as 'less than'.

Another tiny form of resistance for Jeanette is to push back against the limited tick-box ethnicity options on official forms and questionnaires. She has never seen her own heritage represented on any form, and as almost all forms describe mixed identity as white plus any other minority, she has scant options. So, which box she chooses to tick changes every time.

'I always make a point of ticking as many of those boxes as possible, just to fuck things up for them,' she said, laughing anarchically. 'Particularly when I was younger, I used those boxes as my mini-version of political warfare. I would tick all sorts.

'Now, I tick multiple boxes. I will tick "mixed", "other", sometimes "Black other" as well, and then I will also specify and write out my heritage whenever possible. Because when they put "Asian" on these forms, I know they don't mean *my* Asian.

'With any experience – the Black experience, the white experience, the mixed experience – it is so important to remember that these are not just one thing. One person can't speak on behalf of an entire group simply because they happen to look similar. That is expected with white people; they are treated as individuals, but for some reason there is still a tendency to treat people from ethnic minorities as a collective group, all lumped together.

'We need to get to the point where we can speak about identity in terms of individual, unique experiences, rather than as a collective.'

Mixed people, like Jeanette, who don't have that obvious and visible link to whiteness – who happen to have dark skin or unplaceable physical features – are hastily and carelessly brushed out of the picture. Jeanette doesn't possess the privileges that come with lighter skin, looser curls and Eurocentric features, but she is still a part of the mixed experience. It's vital not to let the hierarchies of whiteness dictate which stories are more worthy of being told.

'We have to find a way to talk about race in a more considered, nuanced way,' Jeanette told me. 'If we can do that, it will always be a more productive conversation. But at the moment, we are so limited in the ways we think about and talk about race. And, in the West at least, there is definitely this binary idea that either you're white or you're other.'

Jeanette wants more space to talk about these 'othered' people, the people who exist outside of the orbit of whiteness; people like her and Bilal who are traditionally excluded from the conversation entirely. She believes that until we properly acknowledge this erasure, and the fact that we exclusively talk about race in relation to whiteness, we will never be able to change the way we think about racial hierarchies, and whiteness will always be at the top – crushing every other group beneath it.

The first step to doing this is unlearning the idea that race always exists as a binary; the thinking that says you're either one thing or another. It's a farcical concept that suggests there is some kind of 'racial purity' at either end of the spectrum. It would be easy to believe that the mainstream acceptance of mixed identities undermines this binary – that our very existence suggests it is possible to be something else, to be *both*, to disrupt the idea of 'purity' – but in reality, when so many people still see mixedness only as slotting neatly between Black and white, this limited definition reinforces this binary, rather than disrupting it. And when mixed people are praised and celebrated specifically for their physical and aesthetic closeness to whiteness, it's clear that the hierarchy of white supremacy is still working hard and informing public opinion.

Academics Minelle Mahtani and April Moreno wrote that non-white mixed voices are marginalised in current debates, and 'are not given equal and valuable consideration'. Their essay, which was written two decades ago in 2001, says that there is a common societal perception that the term 'mixed race' always means white and Black, and as a result, anyone outside of this binary is ignored. Twenty years later, the distinct lack of substantial studies and analysis about non-white mixed people, and the lack of discussion in the media and in creative arts, suggests this is still the case.

'In spite of the instability surrounding racial and ethnic categorisation, popular conceptions of "mixed race" remain predominantly characterised in terms of a white–non-white dichotomy[2],' they wrote.

'If we do not begin to assert and give consideration to alternative perspectives on "mixed race", we fall prey to binary traps of categorisation, where a majority "mixed race" group (with some white heritage) exists, and other minority "mixes" find themselves silenced or ignored.'

The essay is sadly prophetic, as this is exactly the situation we find ourselves in today, with whiteness being prioritised and repeatedly centred whenever we talk about mixed experiences and identity. The pair went on to emphasise how important it is to produce theory and analysis that directly relates to people with all kinds of mixes, particularly those who are completely non-white, and this is still something we need a lot more of.

_____

2  Minelle Mahtani and April Moreno, 'Same Difference: Towards a More Unified Discourse In "Mixed Race" Theory', 'Rethiking "Mixed Race"', Pluto Press, 2001

We don't hear anywhere near enough of the diverse stories and perspectives that exist within the varied sphere of mixedness – the stories that challenge our conceptualisation of being mixed and can offer valuable alternative understandings.

The erasure of non-white mixed people is nothing new. For decades, the way people have spoken about mixedness has centred whiteness and sidelined everybody else. Even the laws that were created to prevent interracial marriages pivoted around whiteness. The 'anti-miscegenation laws', as they were known, were laws that made interracial marriages illegal in Jim Crow America up until the late 1960s, but they actually only specified that other races couldn't marry *white people* – in many cases they were even more specific and stated that Black people couldn't marry white people. The aim was, more often than not, to prevent relationships between white women and Black men[3]. Two people of different races who weren't white could have been married during that time and it wouldn't have been illegal. And, though it would have raised eyebrows, it probably wouldn't have been vehemently opposed. What this tells us is that it was never the interracial element of these unions in itself that was the problem, it was simply the threat to whiteness.

Decades after the abolition of those laws in the US, Jeanette says she saw a similar level of apathy in the attitudes towards her own parents. It worked in their favour that they were both simply seen as 'other', because they faced less hostility and were in some ways able to fly under the radar as an interracial couple. At the same time, though, this apathy reinforces the exclusion of non-white people from the narrative of mixedness.

---

3   Kenneth James, Lay, 'Sexual Racism: A Legacy of Slavery', National Black Law Journal, Vol. 13, Issue 1, 1993

'I've seen the racism that has affected my parents – both sides – and it is different,' said Jeanette. 'My mum is Filipino, but people just assume she is Chinese, or any kind of Asian really, and people just make these sweeping microaggressions and stereotypes. And for my dad, as a Cameroonian Black man, he faced the same and worse. And he had to deal with a double prejudice because he is also disabled.'

Jeanette's parents met in hospital. After a catastrophic car accident in Cameroon, doctors told Jeanette's dad that he would be paralysed from the neck down. His family didn't accept this diagnosis and sent him to England for a second opinion and treatment. Her mum was working at the hospital where he was recovering and helped nurse him back to health. In time, and after multiple surgeries, the original diagnosis was proved wrong and Jeanette's dad was able to walk again, but he was permanently disabled, and needed a wheelchair and then crutches to get around.

'Neither of them talk about this time much, or what they went through and what they faced, but I can only imagine what it must have been like for them in the 1970s and 1980s in the UK. Immigrants, ethnic minorities, disabled, *and* in an interracial relationship.

'But my mum has told me that people didn't put them under too much scrutiny as a couple because they were both of colour. If they had been white and Black, I think it would have been a different thing, a harder thing. It always seems to be much more of a problem if a person of colour is with a white person. For my parents, I don't think they are even necessarily seen as an "interracial" couple in the same way that couples with one white partner are.

'It's the same school of thought that can mean mixed-race people who aren't part-white are removed from the mixed experience. If you're not affecting whiteness in any way, if you're not in that space, then you're not even counted.'

Bilal works as a diversity and inclusion officer. His whole job is teaching people about their biases and helping them to revaluate their own perceptions. He says the majority of people, white people, are defensive, reluctant, and fearful of talking about ethnicity and racism. He's prepared for the hostility when he opens up these conversations, he expects it now, and it reminds him how limited so many people still are in their understanding of how the social constructions of race impact society. This is why he believes it's so important to continue to expand what we know about issues of ethnicity and racism, and how we talk about it. He says a huge part of that is opening up who we include in these conversations. Talking about mixedness only as it relates to people mixed with white will never improve our understanding; it only shuts people out.

'If we only recognise one type of mixedness, we're going to miss a lot in terms of the conversation,' Bilal told me. 'And it will be kids who miss out on that. When you think about representation in the media, there are a lot of mixed families on TV – which is cool in some ways – but it's always the one type of mixedness that is being presented. So, there is something missing, which is a whole identity for kids growing up who still don't see themselves. They see something that is as close to them as possible, but it is still not them.

'In terms of that legitimacy and validity for kids who are growing up now, I think it's so important to start proactively changing that narrative, so we don't look around in forty years and realise that there are still no books, or studies or works of art about people like us.'

The popularisation of terms like 'BAME', 'people of colour'

and 'women of colour' shows how people who are not white are consistently lumped together, homogenised and stripped of their individual identity. Even though that is not always the original intention of these terms, when they are co-opted by white people and used as a lazy way to signal 'other', these collective terms reinforce the idea of white as the baseline, the norm. The defining attribute of every other ethnic group on the planet becomes the fact that they are not white.

We do the same for mixed groups when we assume 'mixed' means one thing – mixed with white. By homogenising this diverse and wildly varied group into a singular experience, we send a message to people like Bilal and Jeanette that their stories and their experiences are not valid, are not worthy of discussion. Our worth as mixed people shouldn't be dependent on how close we come to somebody else's 'ideal' blueprint of mixedness, a blueprint that has been designed with a focus on proximity to whiteness, a Meghan Markle idealisation. There are so many different stories that need to be told, and only if we can disentangle ourselves from whiteness will they finally have the space to be heard.

We must not forget that there is also complexity when you fall at the other end of the spectrum. Those who are mixed, but appear white, are also frequently excluded from conversations about mixedness. Finding a space for their narratives – for those who 'pass' as white – is important, but it also holds complexities because that discussion must also include an exploration of privilege.

# Chapter 6

# The 'Privilege' of Mixedness and Passing

Depending on what shift I'm working, I either hit Finsbury Park Station with the 6 a.m. or the 7 a.m. crowd. I prefer the 6 a.m. crowd: the women who skip breakfast wearing harassed facial expressions and Lycra and trainers under their professional-looking coats, labourers in paint-flecked work clothes downing Red Bull, elderly people who are losing the ability to sleep so start their days in the middle of the night. Everyone moves a touch slower, there aren't as many people to knock into you. The anxious, frenetic commuter energy that fizzes to a peak at around 8 a.m. is still simmering at a minimum.

It's a freezing December morning. In quieter parts of the city, the ground would still be shimmering with a paper-thin layer of frost, but the all-night footfall of Stroud Green Road means the dampness is never given its moment to crystallise, so the pavement has a cold, wet gleam.

I'm late, so I break into a trot and swing round the corner toward the ticket barriers, my backpack veers out wildly as I make the turn – it contains my trainers, my lunch, two books that I'm not really reading, and my entire make-up bag, so it's essentially a weapon. I bump slightly into a man's shoulder and shoot him an apologetic look, but I don't have time to slow down. I'm in my zone. My headphones cradle my ears in a sound-cancelling caress, whispering the latest episode of the *This American Life* podcast directly into my brain. I'm holding my phone with my thumb hovering, poised to connect to the station Wi-Fi, my bank card is in my other hand to make sure my ticket barrier transition is unimpeded. This is not my first commuting rodeo.

Out of nowhere, a tall Black guy is in my space. Too close. I think he's wearing a dark tracksuit. He's maybe in his forties. He appears almost right in front of me, but I sidestep him without breaking my stride, feeling his eyes climbing every inch of me. I pull at my pleather skirt to make sure it hasn't ridden up at the back.

I don't stop moving, but I haven't shaken him. Now he's backpedalling – quite literally jogging backwards – to stay in my eyeline. He's mouthing something at me. I keep looking down, but he becomes more insistent. He gestures at my headphones and steps in my path again. Finally, I stop, sigh, and reluctantly push my headphones halfway off one of my ears; I look at him with my eyebrows raised and a 'Well, go on then' expression.

'Beautiful, you're looking good this morning, still. You should smile more though,' he says slowly with a languid North London accent. He's licking his lips and trying to pin me to the spot with the ferocity of his eye contact. I don't give him the chance to say more. I grimace in response and step around him; I don't have time for this, I can't miss my tube.

'Mongrel,' he spits as I pass him.

I spin around and stare at him, unsure if I heard correctly. His face has transformed into a sneer of disgust and he's looking at me with barely contained rage.

'Well, you are a fucking mongrel,' he repeats. He doesn't move and neither do I. We stare at each other and I feel a cold wave of fear and anger trickle from my scalp, coating my skin. The sun won't be up for hours, and there aren't enough people around. He's a big guy, and right now he's looking at me as though he wants to hurt me, so I say nothing. I push my headphones back on, turn my back on him, tap through the barriers and go to work.

I think later about his use of that word, how specific it was, and how close to the surface. He was so ready to use my mixedness against me the moment I didn't respond to his advances, so ready to let me know that he didn't see me as Black.

In that situation, a white guy might have called me the N-word, or a 'Black bitch' (as I was called in Paris the summer before, again for not reciprocating some guy's romantic advances to his satisfaction). But 'mongrel' is almost the opposite of this. Tracksuit guy wanted me to know that he specifically saw me as *not* Black. It's a reminder that I will never pass, in either direction. He saw me as neither and he wanted me to know that was a bad thing.

Passing, in this context, refers to racial passing. It is the phenomenon where ethnic minorities can be perceived as white by the wider world. It happens to light-skinned, monoracial minorities who tick those aesthetic markers of whiteness (from skin colour to hair texture to body shape to eye colour), but it also happens to mixed individuals who have one white, or partially white, parent.

The whole idea of passing as white shows up the fallacy of race, and the laughable frailty of its entire construction. The fact that people of different racial groups have the ability to be unquestioningly accepted as white, based on nothing more than their external appearance, surely shows up the superficiality and instability of racial categories. If racial lines can be so easily and imperceptibly crossed in this way, how can anyone argue that there is anything essential or fundamental in your being that makes you Black or white or anything else? The concept of passing as white shows, again, that race really comes down to little more than how you're perceived in any given social setting.

My face is an acutely obvious mixture of both of my parents. I'm a walking homage to the pair of them. Wherever the light hits me, my parents' features burst, kaleidoscopic, onto my own. The generations that came before me tip my eyebrows slightly off balance, plump my bottom lip, stretch my forehead towards the heavens, bake my skin.

To look at me or my little sister, you would probably be able to guess that we have one white parent and one Black parent. At different angles, and at different points in our lives, we have looked like both of our parents – despite looking quite different from each other – and every year brings a clearer point of recognition. We are morphing into them, from the combination curl pattern of our hair, to our build and body types, right down to our smack-bang-in-the middle light brown skin tone. If you were to ask most people in the UK to describe a mixed woman, they would probably describe a face that looks a bit like either of ours. We look exactly how most people would expect us to, slotting neatly into the limited, mainstream understanding of what it means to be mixed – the 'right kind of mixed' – and the limited (often problematic) understanding of how race works aesthetically.

'Have you got some Jamaican in you?' men (always Black men who see my mix more clearly) have asked me countless times, sometimes romantically followed up with, 'Would you like some more?' My visual mixedness, with its diluted but distinct Blackness, its simultaneous proximity to and distance from whiteness, has always been apparent. I have never, could never, and would never want to 'pass' as white. But we don't have any control over that. And the random assignment of hand-me-down attributes we're gifted at birth can create radically different results, even between siblings.

Why does that matter? In the fundamental sense, it doesn't. It changes nothing about our biological make-up, nothing about who we are as people – other than simply how we look – because again, race is *social*, not scientific. The physical attributes we ascribe to Blackness or whiteness are determined by societal groupings, not biological ones. But it does matter; of course it matters, because how you look according to these socially determined racial categories has a direct impact on how you are treated and your ability to have a safe and successful life in this country. It is the reason why my life is in so many ways easier than darker-skinned minorities, and in many ways harder than white people's, if we are to lay it out with facetious simplicity.

So, to be born white passing is to be born into privilege. It means you're able to access layers of society that are closed off to people who don't pass, to people who are more visibly 'other'. But it's far more complex than this – the privilege you can access if you 'pass' depends on so many contextual factors, such as your location, your age, who is judging whether or not you 'pass', and that privilege often comes with a price.

The wider context of racial passing is deeply embedded in American history. From the post-slavery years to the beginnings of the civil rights movement in the 1960s, racial passing allowed light-skinned and biracial Black Americans to access the privileges associated with being white, from education to career prospects, to the healthcare you could receive, to whom you were allowed to marry[1]. The history of the term

---

1 Sinead Moynihan, 'Passing into the present: Contemporary American fiction of racial and gender passing', Manchester University Press, 13th September, 2010

'passing' stems from the nineteenth-century where it was first used to refer to slaves with light skin who escaped to freedom by claiming a white identity.

Sociologist Nicole Rousseau unpacks the connotations of the word really well:

'The vivid language of the term itself evokes many images: passing one's self off as white; choosing to pass over into white society; the passing away of a person's black identity, reborn as white.'[2]

Nowadays, there is a narrative that passing is always a conscious decision, a deception. This negative perception is stoked by contemporary figures who have shot to infamy by 'reverse passing' or 'passing down' – those white people who make headlines when it is revealed they have been claiming (and often profiting from) a Black or ethnic minority identity. And, historically, there are many stories of light-skinned Black and mixed Americans running off to live as white to escape the conditions associated with living as Black in America during this period, and the people thought to have done this are often derided, scorned or criticised for making this decision, for abandoning their people, for 'betraying' their own heritage. But this is often a view that ignores the historical context of the time.

'Historically racial passing from black to white resulted from the social and cultural and legal oppression of white rule . . . "free" African Americans still often felt forced to pass if they could, decades after the abolition of slavery. They were still living under a codified and constitutionally sanctioned system of white supremacy and racial segregation that continued to define their lives, run on the same assumptions about identity

2 Nicole Rousseau, 'Passing'. In G. Ritzer (ed.), The Blackwell Encyclopedia of Sociology, 2007

as the slavery era,[3]' explains Lipika Pelham in her fascinating deep dive into the history of passing.

When you take this context into consideration, passing has always been so much more complex than a temporary disguise or a desire to create a new definition of the self. When we are talking about people from racial minorities passing as white, it was almost always about survival at any cost. It was a destructive and pervasive symptom of white supremacy that stripped people of their identities, histories and family connections, and forced them into hiding in plain sight.

In the twentieth century, writers and creatives became preoccupied with the concept of passing across racial lines as a way of exploring the meaning of identity and belonging. 'Passing' was even a popular film genre in Hollywood for a time, in the 1930s to 1950s when segregation was still a dominant force in American life. John Stahl's 1934 black-and-white adaptation of Fannie Hurst's novel *Imitation of Life* may have been the most successful of these – there was such a hunger for the narrative, the film was even remade in 1959. We have already touched on the reductive, damaging portrayal of the mixed protagonists in narratives of this sort – the 'tragic mulatto' – but I mention it again here to provide a reminder of how recently passing as white was pathologised like this on mainstream platforms. The fascination with this concept persists today. In 2021, Nella Larson's 1929 novella *Passing* was adapted for the big screen with a debut at the Sundance Film Festival.

Today, passing is generally more incidental. It happens to you because of the way that race is visually coded and how you are perceived. It is much less likely to be an active

3   Lipika Pelham, 'Passing an Alternative History of Identity', Hurst & Company, 2021

decision to conceal your heritage, particularly in the UK, where the one-drop rule (the American-born idea that 'one-drop' of Black blood makes you Black) has never been quite so vehemently implemented. The concept of passing is also much wider now than the Black/white binary understanding that used to dominate the phenomenon. Being perceived to pass as white is something that can affect multiracials of any mix, as long as they tick those visual markers of whiteness.

These days, people are much more likely to have passing thrust upon them, and it can be a fine line to walk between acknowledging and utilising the privilege that comes with being perceived as white, and the need for belonging and acceptance within your minority heritage. Speaking to mixed people who pass as white, some told me that passing can constitute a painful and damaging erasure of their ethnicity. And, far from trying to use the privilege of whiteness to their advantage, some end up overcompensating to 'prove' that they aren't white, or to justify their self-identification as mixed.

In a 2007 American sociology study looking at mixed women and privilege, Silvia Chritina Bettez calls her multi-racial participants 'border crossers'. She says they are 'both uncomfortable admitting participation in the culture, yet also able to recognise its power . . . [they] occupy a dual position of operating both within and outside of the culture of power in relation to race.'[4]

This discomfort with presenting as white doesn't come from nowhere. There is a judgement that comes from some if you are

---

4  Silvia Cristina Bettez, 'Secret Agent Insiders to Whiteness, Mixed Race Women Negotiating Structure and Agency', a dissertation submitted to the faculty of the University of North Carolina at Chapel Hill, 2007

seen to be actively trying to pass as white – and sometimes this can spill over even when passing is unintentional and unwanted. In a 2016 study into multiracial Latinxs, author Emily Nanea Renteria says there is an 'outmoded notion that the passer is a con fraught with insecurity, prone to identity crisis, who is disloyal to his or her "true" racial self'. She adds that this negative judgement towards people who pass as white 'serves only to further pathologise multiracial people's autonomy over their own self-identification.'[5] To me, this suggests there is an inherent suspicion of people who pass as white, as though they are trying to manipulate their privilege and play the system to their advantage. This suspicion can make it hard for people who pass to lay claim to their own identity, or to find a space in which they truly feel as though they belong.

Existing in the ambiguous space of mixedness presents a whole range of complexities and unchartered experiences. Existing in that space while being wrongly assumed to be white adds another layer of uncertainty to navigate. The unquestionable privilege that presenting as white provides doesn't necessarily relieve the internal contradictions that many white-passing multiracials live with.

Anna is Japanese and Chinese on her mother's side. Her father is white with Scottish and American heritage. Anna's mum moved to London from Japan, in 1981 when she was twenty-four. Eventually, she settled in Clapham and was introduced to her future husband, Anna's dad, by a mutual friend – and then they discovered they lived opposite one another. They fell in love over music. Anna's mum had taught herself

---

5    Emily Nanea Renteria, 'Pochos/as push back: Multiracial Latinos/as, white passing, and the politics of belonging', thesis, San Francisco State University, 2016

English as a child by translating liner notes in records, and the pair bonded over bands they loved. All of Anna's childhood memories are set to music.

For her mum, music was a gateway to the West. After Japan became a main base for the American military, Anna's mum would search for the radio networks the American soldiers were listening to. At eight years old she would hide the radio under her pillow and listen to the latest Elvis Presley or Monkees hits in the dead of night. She fell in love with American music three years before any hits made it to their shores by official channels.

Music was the bridge that connected the different elements of Anna's family while she was growing up. It softened and dissolved differing perspectives, filed down the rough edges of cultural dissonances. Soft guitar strings spanned oceans and continents. The melodic, easy listening of the 1970s yacht rock that her mum loved, and her dad's collection of punk rock, have served as universal pillars of understanding, even when language and cultural barriers have threatened to trip them up. Anna says music was one of the key forces that brought her mother to the UK in the first place.

Anna's mum was raised as entirely Japanese, with her Chinese heritage discreetly kept in the background. Anna told me that this was because Japan is still a largely 'culturally homogenous' society, and in 1956, when her mum was born, it would have been tough for her and her family if people had known she had different heritage, particularly Chinese or Korean. It was her mother's protection strategy, a different form of passing.

As a result, Anna's mum never wanted her daughter to have to hide any part of herself because she knew what can be lost when you do that.

'My mum wanted me to know my own heritage, to know about Japan, because she always felt hard-done by, not being able to delve into that side of herself.'

Anna's mum is sixty-three and has been in the UK for four decades – the majority of her life – but she has never fully naturalised as British. She still has Japanese citizenship (where it's illegal to have dual nationality after the age of twenty-two), and she made the active choice to keep the country she now calls home at arm's length. Anna says she thinks that decision is about forging and maintaining a sense of identity.

'When she first came here – it was 1981 – she experienced a lot of racism. She was kicked on a bus, called a "Jap" to her face, and as recently as the early 2000s told to "go back to her country" by what appeared to be a middle class white woman near Anna's school. She came to England thinking everything would be fine, but I think these experiences cemented in her mind just how different she is.

'She also effectively lost half of her heritage. She wasn't ever able to explore her Chinese side, she never met her Chinese family, and she was never allowed to learn Chinese. She had a very unusual upbringing because of this obscured heritage. So, despite how long she's been in the UK, I think keeping hold of her heritage, even in the smallest sense, is integral to her perception of her own identity.'

Anna knows how that feels. She says being white-passing has challenged her own sense of identity throughout her life. To look at Anna, you would probably assume she's white, unless she told you otherwise. She has light skin, straight, light brown hair with blonde highlights. Out of everyone else she knows who has one Asian parent, she says she looks much whiter than all of them. But the way she looks is incongruous with the way she feels about herself, her inner perception of who she is.

'I *feel* so Asian,' she told me. We met on a wintery mid-morning in the vast atrium of my office building, a crystalline sky throwing cold sunlight onto us from the glass ceiling high above our heads. We sat opposite each other at a table, Anna cradling a coffee in her hands, blinking slightly sleepily against the brilliance of the day. She was fresh from a stint of night shifts in a hectic newsroom with another one on the horizon, which is the only reason we could meet in the middle of the day on a Tuesday.

'I know *so* much about my heritage. I studied Politics and International Relations at university and specialised in East Asian policy − that is my niche as a journalist, that is what I want to do. But I feel like I'm constantly having to battle for the credibility to be able to do that.'

She finds it frustrating. It feels as though people are constantly questioning who she is, undermining the very core of her existence. It doesn't matter that she can talk to them about detailed Japanese politics or cultural nuances for hours, she still doesn't fit into the tick-box of what they consider to be Asian.

'As problems go, it's pretty minor,' Anna admitted. She did this a lot; this kind of qualification preceded every divulgence of difficulty or complexity in her life. I wanted to tell her that she didn't need to, that the struggles she faces are valid even if she does possess some privilege. And she is acutely aware of this privilege, both in terms of her proximity to whiteness and in her comfortable upbringing. But the privilege of certain aspects of her life doesn't take away the lasting impacts of her lived experiences. The two things can exist simultaneously.

'In terms of my view of myself, passing has been a source of great discomfort and low self-esteem. It's a lot easier to be confident when you know who you are. And people validate that for you from the outside.'

That external validation has been lacking in Anna's life. She said she has always struggled to fit into groups and find her place in the world. She wasn't Japanese enough, she didn't fit in with other mixed kids because they saw her as white, but she definitely didn't feel white, either. I tried to imagine what it would be like if nobody saw me in the way in which I perceive my own identity, what effect that would have on my sense of belonging. It is yet another layer of complexity that is an integral part of the mixed experience for many.

'It doesn't help that I speak the way that I do, and I went to the school that I went to. I'm perceived as basically a posh white girl who has no problems. And I get that! Comparatively, I completely understand why someone would think that. But that doesn't mean that I'm not who I am, that I don't have these other layers to my identity that aren't apparent in what you see in my face.'

This dissonance feels additionally complicated because Anna's Japanese heritage is so rooted in her beliefs and experiences. Her Asian history is not incidental or ornamental, it was an intrinsic influence in the formative years of her life. Anna's grandmother moved in with her family when she was five years old. She grew up under the influence of two dominant Japanese matriarchs, and it had a deep impact on her sense of identity and the perception of her own ethnicity.

'I spoke Japanese first, before I spoke English. I went to nursery not speaking a word of English,' she said, adding that it didn't affect her ability to catch up academically with her peers. 'I felt very Japanese for a really long time.'

Anna wasn't white-passing when she was a kid. That's in part because she says she used to look more visibly, stereo-typically, Asian. But it's also because she acted Japanese. Her

otherness was overt and unavoidable, more in her mannerisms and behaviours than in the way she looked. She says she
experienced more racism and overt microaggressions during
this time in her life. It was the small stuff that has stuck with
her. Kids would laugh at the incredible bento boxes her mum
made her for lunch and tease her about her 'weird' food.

'I feel completely awful about this now,' she said, cringing
into her seat at the memory. 'My mum would slave away at
these incredible lunches for me, pour so much love into them,
and I came home and said I didn't want them. I asked her
to make me cucumber sandwiches. I don't even like to think
about how horrible that must have been for her.'

She thinks her mum found things like this really difficult,
that she saw it as a rejection of her culture. But seven-year-
old Anna could only think about making her life in the playground as simple as possible. There was bigger, cultural stuff
too – the traditional closer-than-close relationship between a
Japanese mother and her daughter, and the way British children seemed to act more mature much earlier than Japanese
children. Anna felt like she existed in this other, separate world
to most of her friends.

'My mum wanted the best for me, and she really tried to
not expose me to bad things. I would watch Japanese cartoons
and read Japanese comic books. I would go to school and
all the kids would be talking about S Club 7, and I would
be like – what the hell is an S Club 7? I remember Avril
Lavigne being this *thing* that I just didn't understand. So,
I bought into Avril Lavigne really, *really* hard to kind of
overcompensate.

'I had to play catch-up a lot of the time. A lot of the
cultural things that were happening were just completely alien
to me.' She says this barrier to everyday references, coupled

with looking different, speaking a different language and eating different food, made it easy for the other kids to pick on her and isolate her.

'What I find totally bizarre, and totally vindicating, is that it is so *cool* to be into Japanese stuff now.'

These childhood struggles of identity feel familiar to me, but listening to Anna's adult experiences, I became acutely aware that I don't know what it's like to pass, to be presumed to be one of the majority when you walk into a room. My skin tone, my hair texture, my facial features are unavoidably 'other', and despite the privilege I am afforded in certain situations, Anna's stories make it clear to me how the privilege of mixedness operates on a sliding scale of proximity to whiteness. And yet, both Anna and I have one white parent and one non-white parent. It is hard to comprehend that despite this similarity, our experiences of being racialised can be so wildly divergent. We are both mixed, with half of our heritage rooted in whiteness, but we are perceived so differently. It reminds me again how the very concept of passing upends our social understanding of 'race' and the superficiality of how we have decided race works on a visual level.

'Passing works as a prism,' explains academic and author Allyson Hobbs. 'It refracts different aspects of what we commonly think of as racial identity and reveals what is left once the veil of an ascribed status is stripped away. Behind that veil what we know as "race" is simply the lived experience of a people, expressed perhaps as an ache for family and interconnections or sometimes as a longing for music, humor and food. Thus, passing unmasks race as conventionally understood.'[6]

---

6  Allyson Hobbs, 'A Chosen Exile: A History of Racial Passing in Ameri-

Anna would never be called a 'mongrel' in the street, and she is incredibly grateful for this. But, while being hypervisible in your mixedness can present the opportunity for hostility, the lack of visibility that Anna faces can create a whole different set of issues.

Like me, Anna is a journalist, and she's toughing it out in the unrelenting brutality of broadcast newsrooms. She often pitches stories about Japan, but her ideas have a tendency to fall on deaf ears. Having worked in newsrooms, I know that rejection of story ideas is part of the game – particularly for junior producers – but after pitching three Japanese stories and being passed over for each one, Anna began to suspect something more troubling was going on.

'One was a Japanese whaling story, another was a mass stabbing in Japan, in a particular area that I was quite familiar with,' she explained. 'I understand that I'm doing other stuff and it could come down to workload, but, surely out of everybody on the team, I'm the most qualified to do said stories? I couldn't understand it.'

She later realised that the senior people didn't realise that she was Japanese. She was being passed over, she believes now, because it was assumed that she didn't have a personal connection with the stories or specialised knowledge in that area because of how she looks.

'I've never made a secret of it,' she said. 'I have even made a big point of saying that I speak the language, that I know the area, that I'm interested in the region generally.

'So, again, they haven't put me in that box because of my appearance. I have to constantly fight for recognition in that space. But also, because I don't fit in that box, I feel they haven't tried to find out what I'm interested in and what I can offer. They put me in the camp of just another white producer who comes from a good school.

'For me, that encapsulates, professionally, a problem that I encounter and will most likely encounter from now on. Which is frustrating.'

It's frustrating, definitely, but Anna knows that being assumed to be a white woman from a good school isn't damaging in most situations – it's often helpful. The privileges that come with proximity to whiteness sometimes overwhelm Anna with guilt, particularly when she thinks about her family. Anna has an incredibly close relationship with her mother, so to see how differently she is treated, how much easier her own life is, how much less open hostility she has to face, feels unbearably unfair.

'For a long time, I didn't even really realise that I was white-passing. I didn't get it because when I look at my face in the mirror, I see my mum.

'I'm related to her. We're the same! I *feel* like we're the same, but I don't have to deal with half the crap that she does, and it makes me feel so guilty. My experiences of explicit racism are virtually non-existent. I am exceptionally lucky. And I feel awful about it. My mum has to deal with so much shit all the time, and I don't.'

She notices it the most when people assume her mum isn't her mum. This is something that happens to a lot of mixed people, and my mum was asked, 'Whose baby is this?' when she was out with me or my sister when we were small. However, there is a different dynamic going on when it is the mother who is the clear person of colour with a child who looks white to the rest of the world.

'When I was younger, people would think she was my nanny, which is absolutely horrifying on so many levels, but truly mortifying for my mother.'

Another microaggression that Anna witnesses regularly with her mother is in restaurants. When out for dinner with a parent, you would expect the bill to be handed to the older person at the table. but Anna says the bill always comes to her, even when her mum was the one who asked for it.

'I think it is so disrespectful, and it makes me feel furious. But at this point my mum is just unbothered by stuff like this. Some of these things are so small, almost imperceptible, unless you're looking for it.'

When she was at university, Anna took her mum for a Sunday carvery. She went to the counter and was given an enormous plate of food. Her mum was right behind her and the servers gave her a much smaller plate of food, even though they had ordered the exact same thing,

'I got to the till and looked at our two plates of food and just thought; "Why?"' she said, with an exasperated frown.

'I took the plates back and showed the servers at the counter and they sheepishly put more food on my mum's plate. I want to reiterate that this isn't a *major* thing to have to deal with, I know that. But it is just another of those small instances of being treated differently, better, because I'm assumed to be white.'

Anna says the accumulative effect of these microaggressions build to a point where you question your own sanity. This is a feeling I can certainly relate to. I think of it as racial gaslighting, where you aren't sure if you're overreacting because the microaggressions can be so subtle and so insidious.

'It's like – am I being crazy? Or is this actually happening? And I feel totally helpless a lot of the time, which is where my feelings of guilt really come from. It's all directed towards my mother because I love her more than anything in the world.'

Having privilege doesn't mean you're not allowed to reflect

on the complexities of the position that you hold in the world. Anna is acutely aware of, and vocal about, her privilege – not only in terms of looking white, but also in reference to her family's socioeconomic position and her education – which is something I find hugely refreshing in a world where so few people are capable of acknowledging the fact that they have had a leg up.

To pass as white is to have privilege. It can also be a barrier between your lived experiences and the experiences of the people you are closest to, the people you feel inextricably tied to. Which, as Anna has found, can weigh on you heavily.

George says he sometimes feels this weight too. Alongside the privilege that he knows passing affords him, he says it can also create a level of erasure of his lived experiences – it can leave him feeling as though he is shut out from certain narratives and conversations.

George's mother is white British, and his father is Indian, born in England after his parents left India for London not long after Partition. But you wouldn't immediately guess George's heritage to look at him; to the untrained eye, or even to most trained eyes, George looks white. He has light skin, light brown hair, green eyes, typically Caucasian facial features. He jokes that the only Indian things about his looks are his height and his copious body hair. What makes it more unusual is how different he looks from his older brother. George's brother looks much more visibly South Asian – darker skin, jet black hair, dark eyes.

Passing as white when neither your father nor your brother does has sometimes been complex for George. He moves through the world with the privilege of a white man and has to watch as his brother faces injustices for no reason other than the random aesthetic result of his particular genetic make-up.

The first time I met George, I walked through the lobby at my office and passed right by him because I was looking for somebody more visibly Asian. He's used to that and helpfully waved me over in his direction. In the baby photos he showed me, George is bright blonde and cherubic. He's used to having to explain his heritage, he's used to the surprised expressions and incredulous looks when he tells people he has an Indian father. He's used to the suspicion. He faces these questions with a smile because he knows how race works in terms of the visuals, and aesthetically, he doesn't hit society's quota for mixedness. He doesn't blame people for assuming he is white.

But that doesn't mean it's always easy. At school he was once called a liar – by a *teacher* – because his older brother is so much more visibly Indian than he is. People often wouldn't believe that they were related. He has comforted his parents' after a racist neighbour keyed their car twice in a couple of weeks. He has watched as his dad is stopped by security for 'random' searches at the airport, while he sails through.

Like me, George doesn't love the terminology around this phenomenon, but he recognises that it is currently the most practical phrase to describe what it is. But 'white-passing' inherently suggests that to be white is the correct and default state. The construction of the wording implies some kind of racial test, white is a pass, so everything else is . . . a fail? It's imperfect, and centres whiteness in a way that George doesn't feel reflects who he is.

But what this phrase does do is to reflect the privilege that comes with looking white. You're granted a *pass* to access more of the world, to move through the world with greater ease. Again, though, the lack of consistency makes that privilege hard to measure.

'White-passing is so open to interpretation,' George told me. 'It's about who you actually pass as white *to*. Because it's not always the same. Some mixed people, or people with Indian heritage, might see that I'm also mixed. It's often these people who show no surprise whatsoever when I tell them that I'm half Indian. So, despite how I look, I'm not *always* taken for white. It depends who's seeing me, and in what context.'

The 2016 study into multiracial Latinxs I referenced earlier in the chapter suggests that a large part of the privilege that comes with white-passing stems from the ability to choose. As George has made clear, this is not always the case, but the American study concluded that multiracial people are usually able 'to choose from a range of self-identifications'. The author of the study says the people she interviewed benefit from this 'flexibility' and that racialisation 'did not impact subjects' life chances in a structural sense: 'Whiteness, white ancestry, and white passing provided more flexibility and agency in terms of identity choices than was available to darker-skinned respondents,' read the findings. 'The interviewees were mindful that freedom from racialisation helped them in daily life, whether because of looks or familiarity with white cultural codes.'

George says that it is in public spaces where he feels this kind of privilege the most. He doesn't have to cope with the open racial abuse that his brother and father have had to suffer at the hands of strangers. He is able to move through the world with the privilege of a white man, not other, but one of the majority. He may not feel it, but that is how he appears, and he is quick to acknowledge that there is a safety and ease of public existence that comes with that.

He also raises the interesting point that passing – truly being perceived as white – only really works in public spaces, where it is strangers who are reacting to you. With friends, family and people who know you, they will know your heritage, so you're never passing in private, personal spaces. But even around people who know you, it's easy to not be seen for who you are.

'My friends sometimes forget that I'm not white,' said George. 'People definitely forget that I have this whole other identity. They forget that if they tell a crass joke about something race-related that I'm not going to find it funny.'

In public spaces, George's 'camouflage' of whiteness has also given him disconcerting levels of access to the most hostile opinions about people of colour. He finds that people who hold these views can feel safe to voice them around him. It's an unsettling assumption of complicity that leaves George wondering – how many white people just nod along when they hear things like this, particularly when they don't realise there's a non-white person in their presence?

George was at an England football game a few summers back. At the time, he was working for Kick It Out, an anti-racism in football organisation, so being in the stands was like a second home. He felt comfortable in that environment. The crowd around him was entirely white, and one fan decided it was the perfect opportunity to share his most vitriolic, racist thoughts with everyone within earshot.

'I don't even know why he said this, it wasn't like there were any South Asian players on either team,' George told me. 'Some people in the crowd were singing "I'm England Till I Die", and this guy, who was sat right behind me, yelled; "Yeah, but it's not England is it? It's full of Pakis!"'

'So, I turned around and said, "Don't fucking say that."'

At this point, I tried to picture the scene. George, a head shorter than I am, spinning around in his seat to face a stranger in a crowd full of white men and, without missing a beat, telling him about himself in no uncertain terms. I'm in awe of the reckless bravery of this. I wonder if passing, in this instance, provides a metaphorical suit of armour. As a visibly brown woman alone in a sea of white faces, I'm pretty sure I would have faced the front and kept quiet.

'He then asked me if I was "one of them",' George continued. 'He was basically asking me – why do I care enough to call him out? But I didn't tell him. I said, "It doesn't matter where I'm from, just don't fucking say that." Then he started calling me a "lefty" and a "social justice warrior". I was like – how did you know?!' he laughed. I felt glad he was able to keep a sense of humour about it.

To me, that interaction sounds terrifying, as though George's safety was teetering on a knife edge. But maybe his confidence in this situation is part of his passing privilege, added to the privilege of being male. It almost feels as though he has the ability to infiltrate the 'enemy', to slip below the radar and call people out before they've even realised that he's different to them. But, on the flip side, this level of exposure to hostility and second-hand abuse can be tiring. George doesn't want to fit in with a group that holds negative, damaging beliefs about people like him. It hurts to navigate these interactions, and his ability to blend exposes him to this kind of language on a painfully regular basis.

'People can feel comfortable making racist remarks in front of me because they think I'm the same as them,' George explained. 'Because they see me as a white guy, they think that even if I'm not going to join in and laugh at their comments, I'm not going to say anything or stand up to them. Whereas if I were my brother, these people might be more wary about being so brazen with their racism.'

As much as George understands why people perceive him

as white, it still leaves him with a desire to justify himself, to almost overcompensate to 'prove' his heritage to people. It's a pressure he's felt since he was young. He remembers that at school, in his year, there were maybe fifteen or so visibly South Asian kids, and they would hang out together. He says he wasn't particularly bothered about being part of any kind of clique, but he did feel excluded by them at times.

George's school had a religious assembly every Monday that everyone had to attend. In fact, there were three different assemblies – one for Christians or anyone who was atheist or non-religious, one for Jews, and one for anybody who was anything else: Muslim, Sikh, Hindu, Buddhist, Jain.

'Leaving aside how problematic the "other" group was – putting all those religions in what was effectively a group for all the brown people – it was actually by far the most interesting one to go to,' said George. At school, he spent a year going to the assembly for Christians and athiests because he wasn't religious, so he felt it didn't really matter to him, but one day he decided to go to the 'other' group. Lots of kids who went to this 'other' assembly weren't at all religious – including George's brother – but because they were brown or Black, they weren't questioned about it. But when George turned up, he was met with smirks from the other kids and the teachers told him he had to leave.

George said that part of this small rebellion stemmed from this need to prove his worth, to make a statement that he *was* allowed to be there, that he did have a claim to that space – particularly when he knew so many other kids attended that assembly without any religious affiliation. I can understand this quest for belonging, an innate need to show everyone that you have a right to be somewhere.

'I was trying to make a bit of a point to the teachers because

I knew they would say something about me being there, but I was also, I think, trying to make a point to the other British Asian kids in the school, even if I wasn't exactly clear on that in my own head at the time. Looking back though, I'm sure I wanted to show them that I was allowed to be there, even if I didn't look like I was.'

He sometimes catches himself doing similar things now, as an adult. He says when he meets British Asians through work, he finds himself subtly trying to shoehorn his ethnicity into conversations. He says he feels a need to signal to them that he does have Indian heritage, that they have a shared understanding in that way.

'Maybe I shouldn't feel like I need to do that, or maybe I shouldn't bother doing that, but it is definitely something I have got into the habit of doing,' he added. 'And it can be a bit draining, you know, having to justify my existence in this way.'

George is acutely aware of the powers and freedom that come with appearing white to the outside world. And he knows that no matter how this power may fluctuate depending on circumstance, his life will always be distinctly easier than his dad's or his brother's. He summed it up with characteristic self-awareness:

'Passing as white can be complicated for me. First and foremost, it's absolutely a privilege.

'But there is the other side to it, which is that sometimes I feel the fact that I'm Indian isn't recognised. It's not something that I'm bitter about, or carry around with me every day, and I don't feel like I've been *consistently* excluded from spaces that I have a right to be in. But occasionally I do find myself feeling like I have to explain my existence as a mixed race person, which can be tiring.

'I'm not just a white person, and my life experience is not just that of a white person, because I grew up in a British-Indian home, with lots of Indian family around me, and I'm proud of my Indian heritage.

'That being said, I'm always aware that ultimately my white appearance – certainly in public – affords me more privilege than it does disadvantages.'

The problem with 'passing' is that it's not a steady state, which is another reason why it's difficult to simply say that people who pass have privilege, and people who don't pass, do not. It's too reductive. People who *sometimes* pass as white can't always access those spaces, so the privileges that come with being perceived as white are entirely dependent on who is perceiving you, and reams of contextual factors that are usually out of your control. It's a fluctuating, moveable beast, and the slipperiness of the very concept of passing makes it an unwieldy and unpredictable tool of privilege.

Anna doesn't *always* pass as white. As she told me, when she was younger and more visibly 'other', she experienced more overt racism. But even as an adult, now that her features normally allow her to blend seamlessly in white crowds, her otherness is obvious in some situations, particularly with those who have a more prescriptive, exclusive concept of whiteness.

Anna attended a Russell Group university and during her first term, she had an interaction with another student during a formal hall dinner – a young, white man – that she still can't quite believe.

'I was sitting at the table with this guy, and it was such an inane conversation that I don't even remember the context of how we got there, but all of a sudden, he called me a "Jap",' Anna told me.

'I said, "Excuse me?" and I obviously looked very shocked. His response was something like, "What? Why are you upset?"'

When she was even younger than this, Anna had experiences where friends had used racist language without realising and had been mortified when they discovered it was offensive once it has been explained. So, when she tried the same tactic with the guy at the dinner – of patiently and carefully explaining why 'Jap' was insulting and racist – Anna was baffled when it didn't play out in the way she expected.

'He actually turned to a friend sat next to him – who I believe was either Chinese or from Hong Kong – and asked him, "Oh, but you don't think it's racially insensitive, right?" as though we are all the same. And obviously his poor friend was in an impossible situation and just went along with him and was like, "Er . . . no, it's not that bad."

'At this point I'm getting quite exercised, and quite upset to be honest. I have never had someone actively disagree with me when I've told them that something is racially insensitive. What made it even worse was this kind of boy's club mentality all around me. Another friend of mine, who was sat near, then starts to kind of wind me up saying; "Oh, are you going to cry now? Is there really any point getting upset about this? Are you going to cry?"

'The whole thing was so shocking to me. We were all around nineteen at this point, adults really. These are incredibly well-educated people, and it was only a few years ago. Ignorance just can't be an excuse in this case.' Anna smiled and delivered her killer 'fun fact' about this anecdote: the guy who called her a 'Jap' ended up associated with right wing politics after this incident.

The stories from people who pass as white further highlight just how varied and context-dependent the mixed experience is. George and Anna have completely different heritages, backgrounds, upbringings, genders, and as such they move through the world differently. They interpret their own racial identities differently. And yet, there are overlapping traits that tie their narratives together: the ways in which they navigate the complexities of their privilege, the guilt they feel at witnessing the struggles of minority family members, the disconnection between how they look and how they feel about themselves.

It's easy to dismiss the experiences of white-passing multiracial people as unimportant. If you move through the world as white, what can there be to complain about? What can there be to discuss? It's true that the ability to blend in with the majority and reference your minority heritage only when you choose to make it known are benefits that most people of colour can never experience. But both Anna and George have provided a glimpse into the often-ignored intricacies of passing and the nuances of the aesthetic markers of race.

Their heritage is within them, it's in their home, in their memories with their family, in their own understanding of who they are, that shouldn't be diminished simply because their outward appearance doesn't fit the societal description of their racial category. They have a right to be seen and acknowledged as who they know themselves to be, with an understanding that the 'privilege' of passing as white is not fixed or standardised.

It reminds me, once again, that the perceived privilege of mixedness is a sliding scale with whiteness at the top, and everybody else underneath. Like Anna and George, I have more privilege in certain contexts thanks to my proximity to whiteness. But the level of privilege we can access is always dependent on who is perceiving us, and where they would place us on this sliding scale. And a privilege that you have such little control over doesn't feel like much of a privilege at all. And it can make navigating the world, particularly professional spaces, incredibly complicated.

# Chapter 7

# Navigating the World and Work

My first national media job was working as a trainee producer in a broadcast newsroom. Newsrooms are notoriously stressful, and this one was no different. Junior producers being screamed at by senior members of staff was a regular occurrence. I was sworn at, accused of incompetence in front of colleagues, yelled at and told that I 'wasn't a grown-up', all within my first few weeks. A senior member of staff even joked – loudly – that myself and another non-white producer should not be sent to a bomb scare because we would 'look like terrorists'.

It wasn't just me. I wasn't exactly a natural in that environment, but I certainly wasn't bad at the job. In that room, someone was always running, shouting, sobbing at their desk, yelling down the phone. People would quit dramatically on the spot. It wasn't unusual to go to the loo and hear someone crying as quietly as they could in the next cubicle. It was the junior staff who bore the brunt of it. For my first six months as a trainee, I had to take a deep, steadying breath before walking through the door every morning, to steel myself against whatever madness awaited me that day.

Then you get used to it. Suddenly you're slightly less junior than you were, and the way people speak to you seems less scary, normal even. It's so easy to be drawn in by the adrenaline, the ego-inflating self-importance of the drama. You can see how people become hardened by it. After the initial fear subsides, working in an environment like that can start to chip away at your sense of what is really important.

I learnt a lot working there. It toughened me up and I don't think starting any new job will ever feel daunting after that baptism of fire. I had incredible experiences and made some truly exceptional friends, but the potential brilliance of the job itself was eclipsed, for me, by the utterly consuming toxicity of the culture. And I put a lot of that down to the complete dearth of diversity. According to data from 2016, journalism in the UK is 94 per cent white, and I felt that, acutely, every day that I worked there.

It's one thing to work a stressful job, it's another thing entirely to work a stressful job and feel as though you don't have *anyone* in your corner – no one to talk to when someone makes a problematic comment in a morning meeting or if someone gets overly handsy with your new box braids; no one willing to get angry with you when the 'BAME' pay gap figures are released and the financial inequalities of the entire institution are laid bare in black and white. Those exceptional friends I mentioned understood, and many of them are still there fighting the good fight, trying to make sure underrepresented voices are heard. But it can't be down to a handful of minorities to shake the tables every single day in the face of silence from the majority. I know that they are exhausted.

Minorities who work in majority-white environments are often plagued with the underlying suspicion of tokenism. It can make you question your legitimacy and your right to even exist in that space – did I get this job simply because I tick a box? I would find myself asking that whenever I was feeling insecure or inadequate which, thanks to a culture of blame and unproductive feedback, happened a lot.

One morning, early in my traineeship, I was asked to give a talk to a visiting group of teenagers from a college in Lewisham – Black, Asian, minority teens from a poor area of London. The visit was part of a scheme that opens up access to otherwise impenetrable professions for economically deprived kids and gives them a taste of what these workplaces might be like.

It was the boss who asked me to do it. One of the big bosses. So, when he perched himself on the edge of my desk, I had a small heart attack and temporarily forgot how to breathe. I'm paraphrasing, but the conversation went something like this:

'Natalie, you're young. There are some young people coming into the newsroom today and I'd love for you to talk to them – tell them about your experiences here, what you love about it, how you got into journalism, that kind of thing,' he said.

'Oh . . . er, sure. Of course. Are you sure I'm the right person?' I asked, relieved I wasn't being summoned for a bollocking.

'I feel like you'll be able to relate to them. Make sure to give a good impression.'

He sauntered away, humming happily to himself, and I sat there trying to unpick the real meaning behind his request.

Was I being asked to talk to these teenagers because I was young? Nope, that wasn't it. I was twenty-seven at the time and there were loads of junior reporters and producers in that room who were younger than me. I was being asked to talk to these teenagers because I have brown skin, because I looked like them, and because there was only ever a handful of people in that newsroom – out of hundreds of employees – who weren't white.

Immediately a conflict kicked off in my mind. On the one hand, I had been noticed by the big boss, he remembered my name and was offering me an opportunity, of sorts. On the same hand, of course I wanted to talk to these kids, of course I wanted to encourage them to go into journalism, to persuade them that we need their stories, that their experiences and perspectives are valid and vitally necessary in the world of news. I had seen how damaging a homogenously white newsroom could be – I was living it – and if there was any way I could influence change and inspire applications from different pools of people, I wanted to grasp that. But, on the other hand, I couldn't shake the nagging suspicion that the whole exercise was really about box ticking.

How could I stand up there and preach the benefits of working in the industry, give tips and advice as though it would be easy for these minority kids to get a foot in the door? The colour of my face spinning them a lie from the very beginning. My brownness telling them, 'Yes, you can do this too', when in reality they would rarely see faces that looked like mine even if they ever managed to get a shift in most newsrooms. How could I persuade them to fight for a place in this industry when I had seen Black and brown employees leaving it in droves after just a few years because they realised that progression after a certain point was near impossible?

And there were layers to the deception. As well as a possible misrepresentation of the make-up of the newsroom, it also felt disingenuous to present myself as a relatable figure. 'I was just like you!' I was meant to tell them, but I never was. My grandparents didn't have much, and on my dad's side they were immigrants – part of the Windrush generation – but my parents pretty much became middle class, and my sister and I definitely are. I went to a grammar school; my dad built a long and successful career in journalism; my social and economic privilege means that my access to these spaces was always going to be so much easier than it could ever be for these kids. Our only similarity, the only thing that makes me relatable to them, is the colour of my skin. 'If I can do it, you can too.' I couldn't get up there and make that promise in good faith. My mixedness plays a part in that as well.

Up until now, everything I've discussed about the workplace also applies for monoracial minorities. The discrimination, microaggressions, lack of representation, barriers to progression – these are all realities of professional life for non-white people in this country. But there is a specific challenge that mixed employees face at work – at least, those of us who are partially white – and that is navigating our palatability.

My mixedness provides a level of diversity that ticks the box without being 'too much'. For bosses, I am an acceptable, *palatable* level of ethnic, a Black woman who doesn't stray too far from what my white employees are able to connect to. A connection that is partly based on the similarities of my education and my upbringing, yes, but is also linked directly to the relative lightness of my skin. My palatability is, I think, the real reason I was asked to speak to those teenagers. It may be the reason I was pedalled out to appear on corporate videos, speak on internal panels, maybe even part of the reason I was in that room in the first place.

It's feels wrong to call this palatability a 'challenge' when it so clearly provides tangible benefits and more opportunities than people who are darker-skinned than I am, but the challenge is that it serves as a reminder that my worth and potential in a professional sense is in some way tied to my visible proximity to whiteness. I think it's possible to simultaneously acknowledge the privilege of this position and the inherent discomfort that comes with directly benefitting from it. It's important to remember that when professional opportunities are dependent on a scale that's based on white supremacy, the only people who genuinely benefit from that system – in a lasting, fundamental way – are white people.

The problem with ticking that box is that it can turn you into the face of an organisation while simultaneously taking away your voice. They want us on their posters, but they don't want to hear from us. And I'm absolutely not here for this meaningless, performative 'diversity'. Neither is Jeanette.

Jeanette has a Filipino mother and a Cameroonian father, and we first met her a couple of chapters back, talking about being mixed without whiteness. So, she doesn't have the same palatability that I do, that recognisable link to whiteness that can put employers at ease. In a professional capacity, she told me this translates as microaggressions, and people struggling to identify where she is meant to 'fit'. She hates the awkwardness of repeatedly explaining her 'non-conventional' mix.

Jeanette is around my age and works in London as a content strategist so, like me, words are her professional currency. And yet, in the workplace, she's found that ethnicity is a subject where people seem to lose their ability to communicate altogether.

'Generally speaking, the people I work with, the white people, don't really know what mixed race is,' said Jeanette. We met on a weekday, snatching an hour between meetings. It was one of those late autumn days that never quite manages to shake off the night before, and 12 p.m. felt like twilight. We hid from the dank darkness in the warm florescence of the office café.

'I don't look identifiably mixed race, as in, what people assume mixed race is. My mix is not white and Black. So, for the most part, people are pretty confused.'

It's the combination of her dark skin and more typically east Asian features, she explained. She told me people have asked her why her eyes 'look Chinese'. Not exactly the best opener for a logical, enlightening discussion about ethnicity, but she prefers questions – even bad questions – to an awkward silence.

'People don't want to talk about race in the workplace,' she added. 'It makes them nervous; I think people are even scared to say the word "Black". So, instead of having those conversations, they make a lot of assumptions because that's easier than actually having to talk about it.'

A recent independent survey about race in the workplace found that 'all BME groups are more likely to be overqualified than White ethnic groups but White employees are more likely to be promoted than all other groups.'[1] But when it comes to progression and opportunities, mixed employees fare much better than most monoracial minorities.

A 2017 study by the Chartered Institute of Professional Development (CIPD) asked people if they felt they had been overlooked for promotion at work – around 24 per cent of white people reported that they felt they had.[2] Mixed employees and Chinese employees were joint second on that scale, with only around 26 per cent saying they felt they had been overlooked. For all other monoracial minorities, that figure quickly jumps up, with much higher proportions of Indian, Pakistani and Black African employees reporting they had been overlooked (around 34 per cent).

So, the direct benefits of this scale of palatability are clear. The study explains that their 'mixed' category is referring to

---

1 'Race at work 2018: McGregor-Smith review - one year on'
2 Chartered Institute of Professional Development, 'Addressing the barriers to BAME employee career progression to the top', 2017

employees who are mixed with white *and* those who don't have a white parent, but I think it is safe to make an educated assumption that colourism plays a big part in why some mixed employees have better career prospects. Aesthetic proximity to whiteness is likely a major factor that gives these mixed employees a 'pass' and contributes to their palatability. But that doesn't apply to people like Jeanette who are mixed without white heritage.

Jeanette's heritage and the mix of her parents' backgrounds is relatively uncommon, unguessable. She's not easily placed and, as a result, she says she feels a sense of unease from people she works with – an uncomfortable uncertainty that leads to a stifling fear of saying the wrong thing.

'Only a few people have ever spoken to me about my mix or said to me, "You look mixed", or, "You look Asian". And those people are always from *ends*, you know, urban areas, inner-city areas, people who have been exposed to more people from different places. They're more used to seeing mixed people, and more comfortable talking about it too.

'Our receptionist is mixed. She's Cypriot and her dad is mixed Jamaican and Chinese. And she has said to me, "Wow, you look just like my family." But, for the most part, people just don't really know. And they're shocked when they find out what my mix is.'

A 2009 study looking at colourism in professional situations found that: 'Light-skinned black males are more likely to assimilate into the work environment, not alienate their clients, and not appear threatening.'[3] It's clear that even monoracial

---

3   Canotal, Eugene Espejo, 'An overseas example of "lighter is better": the implications of colorism among male sex workers in Thailand', Masters Thesis, Smith College, Northampton, MA, 2009

employees who also achieve this aesthetic proximity to white-ness are able to benefit from this sliding scale of palatability, which suggests that it isn't really being *mixed* that provides benefits in the workplace; rather, it's simply about *looking* as white as possible. The darker your skin, the more 'threatening' you will be perceived to be by your employers, which, as Jeanette knows, isn't going to work in your favour when a promotion opportunity pops up.

I have seen first-hand that majority white media institutions are haemorrhaging minority talent. It's these deeply institu-tionalised and impenetrable barriers to progression that leave many people of colour feeling as though they have no option other than to leave. That's certainly how I felt, despite my privilege and my ability to tick a box in a less 'threatening' way, so I can only imagine how hostile these environments must feel for darker-skinned employees like Jeanette.

Jeanette is tired of the assumption that there is only one way to be mixed; that it always has to include whiteness. That you have to be a Meghan Markle doppelgänger in order to tick that box in mainstream understanding. She often feels excluded from the narrative about mixedness, and she thinks it's this lack of understanding that makes it harder for people to have these conversations with her about her heritage. She is too much of an unknown entity.

She told me that we need more space to discuss racial iden-tity in the workplace. She thinks it would help to normalise diversity, and would help minority employees to feel welcome, listened to, and as though they have as much right to exist in those spaces as their white counterparts. It will take difficult and honest conversations to get to that point, but Jeanette is more than willing to be the one to start them.

'As I've got older, I've become more comfortable addressing

things head on. I'll make jokes about it, I'll call people out if they say something racist, I'll tell them that it isn't acceptable.

'You might be the first person of colour that some of your colleagues have ever had to interact with on a daily basis. And I don't mean someone you just say "hi" and "bye" to – this is *real* interaction. We spend more time with our work colleagues than we do with our families. So, it may be the first time that people have ever had the opportunity to *really* get to grips with these issues and ever ask about them.'

The CIPD study mentioned above also found that: 'Significantly more BAME employees overall than white British say their career to date has failed to meet their expectations (40% versus 31%), in particular those from black (44%) or mixed race (42%) backgrounds.' This feels at odds with the study's finding that mixed employees were one of the *least* likely groups to have felt overlooked for promotion – and highlights the problem with lumping all mixed employees together and expecting some kind of cohesion. There is no singular experience of being mixed in the workplace because how you're treated is so often dependent on how you present, visually, and how you are perceived by others as a result. And there is no blueprint for that when you're mixed.

As I spoke to Jeanette – both of us sipping herbal tea and mindlessly overrunning our allotted lunch breaks – I was struck by her optimism. She smiled as she spoke, and as she reflected on her professional life, so much of it was positive, encouraging, hopeful. She balanced any critical remarks with caveats and alternative perspectives, and she was careful not to paint herself as a victim or make any excuses, potentially a trait she inherited from her parents, who instilled a strong belief that she had to make her own way in the world.

'My parents are not only of colour, they're also immigrants.

So they had this mentality that you have to work twice as hard.

'I don't know if that is really true; I don't necessarily believe that to be the case any more. I think people do see others for their merits . . . but it's hard to say because often the bias is so unconscious.'

Jeanette was uncertain as she said this. I got the sense that she wants to see the best in people even despite evidence to the contrary. I asked her about this concept of 'unconscious' bias, and whether giving it that label was an 'easy out', a way of absolving white people of any responsibility when it comes to their own biases. She agreed, but also said that it wasn't always cut-and-dry. There were often concurrent, contextual factors at play when it comes to how you're treated at work, she said; sometimes it's more complex than a simple judgement about your ethnicity.

'It's about being mixed race, it's about race in general, it's class, it's gender – it's an incredibly complicated conversation,' she said.

'It's hard to pinpoint things that have actually happened,' she added, and I nodded with the memories of the many times I have been made to question myself over barely perceptible injustices in the workplace. Was that what I thought it was? Am I allowed to get annoyed?

'Sometimes, you're not sure if it's because you're a different race or if it's because you're junior, or the assistant, or a combination of things. I remember doing an internship at a newspaper and this woman who worked there wouldn't remember my name. She just refused to learn it. It was like something out of *The Devil Wears Prada*; she called me Jasmin for ages. It was so confusing.'

The longer we spoke, the more Jeanette began to peel back the protective layers and expose the rawness underneath.

She spoke about the intangibility of the microaggressions she's faced, the hard to pinpoint and even harder to explain discriminations that she remembers from her relatively short working life, particularly at the beginning of her career when she didn't have the experience or the power to push back against authority figures.

'I remember starting out and doing internships. I was probably the only person of colour. Any colour of any kind. I'm not sure if the people I was working with would have ever felt any kind of way about me, but I felt extremely conscious of existing in an incredibly white space.

'I had this eager to please, prove yourself element to my attitude. I was very aware of not being perceived in a certain way in the workplace. Of not playing into stereotypes. Of not being seen as the "angry Black woman". But now, I don't give a damn.

'They're going to think whatever they think about me anyway, so I'm not going to try to check my behaviour on that basis – because they will make assumptions and judgements regardless of what I do.'

It wasn't easy for Jeanette to reach this level of confidence, both in herself and in a professional capacity, and it certainly isn't easy for minorities to feel emboldened enough to call out mistreatment or discriminatory behaviour in the workplace. Doing that can damage your career prospects, have you blackballed, disciplined, even fired. But Jeanette seems to have found a way to do this effectively. Maybe it's the disarming power of her smile. Or maybe her mixedness plays a part in her workplace empowerment.

Jeanette doesn't have the palatability that comes with proximity to whiteness. She doesn't have that 'non-threatening' tick-box appeal that people who are mixed with a white parent often possess. Despite this lack of relative privilege, there are other things about being mixed that may have helped her feel powerful, and more in control of her situation at work. Top of that list is her ability to code-switch – to adapt her behaviour, thinking, attitudes, even the way she speaks, depending on the environment she is in at any given time. Mixed people have often had more practice at this skill because of the likelihood of being exposed to different cultures, environments and racial categories from an early age.

According to an American study, 19 per cent of multiracial Americans feel their ethnicity is an advantage in their lives, which is significantly more than monoracial Americans – only 4 per cent say the same.[4] It could be that it is this ability to exist and even thrive in multiple spaces that causes mixed people to see their ethnicity as an active benefit. So much of the narrative about being mixed focuses on lacking; on not being enough of either thing, of being 'rejected' by both sides. But what about the flipside of this argument? Being both, rather than neither, might help mixed people to position themselves successfully in multiple settings. Jeanette has certainly found this.

She grew up in Barking, which was then a predominantly white, working-class area. She then went to a secondary school in Newham where most of the kids were of colour. Suddenly, she was surrounded by lots of Black kids, lots of Filipino kids. She became incredibly adept at changing her behaviour depending on the context.

'People of colour code-switch all the time. Growing up, there was no one else who looked like me, but I had to be able to

---

4   Parker, Horowitz, Morin and Lopez, 'Multiracial in America', Pew Research Centre Report, 11th June, 2015

go to the pub and get down with everyone there, then that changed at secondary school, and then that changed again when I started work and had to be able to put my professional hat on.

'You become even more used to code-switching when you're mixed. When you meet your dad's family it's a different thing to meeting your mum's family – and you get really good at adapting to that. And that's something that transfers into professional scenarios too.'

Maybe Jeanette's experience of seamless code-switching gives her an edge in professional environments. She can communicate well in different settings, navigate potential hostility, even speak out against injustice with less fear of ramifications. She also just seems to be great at her job. From what she told me, I got the impression that she is confident, determined, not easily cowed. The flexibility she gains from her mixedness is just one of the many attributes that makes her stand out professionally.

And, of course, code-switching and professional flexibility can only ever get us so far. We are still, most of us, navigating our workspaces as minorities, and shouldering all the bullshit that comes with that. And it isn't only in an office space where we have to code-switch. It is something that is frequently required in educational settings, too. And not everyone can do it successfully.

Bilal, who we met a few chapters ago, and is mixed South Asian and Black Caribbean, struggled to fit in while he was studying at Cambridge. In 2016, only 1.5 per cent of full-time students at Cambridge were Black; Bilal graduated a few years before this, and these figures are an improvement on the diversity stats from his time there. It was an environment that felt entirely alien to him, and he struggled to cope in the early months.

'I grew up in very Black spaces. I went to a Black church, most of my friends are Black, and I grew up around Black people. I grew up in Brent and it was such a multicultural place, and at the time it was pretty much just Asian and Black people, there wasn't really anyone else.

'When I got to Cambridge and it was a sea of white faces, that was a real culture shock. I was like – woah, white people are *here*. I knew they existed in the country, but I didn't know they were literally all in one place like this.'

Bilal said adapting to that environment was hard. He was very much seen as 'other' from the very beginning, and unlike Jeanette's experience, this mythical power for seamless code-switching that mixed people are supposed to possess never materialised.

'The music that people were listening to was not music I would ever listen to, and their food was dry and unseasoned. Fresher's Week was *long*, I'll just say that. I didn't know what was happening.' Bilal laughed as he told me this, but this wasn't a surface-level joke, this one ran deep. To suddenly become one of very few people of colour after existing entirely in diverse spaces up until that point was difficult to get his head around. And, Bilal told me, the white students couldn't get their heads around him, either.

In his first week, a guy knocked on Bilal's door, having never met him before, and asked him if he sold weed. And that was his first indication of how these white teenagers saw him.

'There was a lot of curiosity from some people,' he explained. 'Some immediately wanted to make friends with me. But it felt like they were thinking, "Wow, I've never had a brown friend before." And there were a lot of people who assumed that I was going to be "cool" – I mean, I am,' Bilal laughed again, 'but why do you think that before even talking to me? Then on the other side of it, there was a total ignorance.

'I felt lost for a while, for a good while. I didn't know any of the customs or the cultures. I was just trying to be a nice person, make friends. And I did make friends, but it took a good six weeks of basically being in shock.'

This feeling was the exact reason Bilal had been reluctant to go to Cambridge in the first place. To cope, he came home a lot – every weekend – during those first few months. Eventually, he forced himself to spend the weekend there, and he finally met some other Black and mixed people through the Cambridge African Caribbean Society. They told him about a road just off campus that would come to make him feel more at home in this strange, white world.

'It's literally just this one road, not far from the university, but you go down it and suddenly there are boss man corner shops, and you can buy plantain. It sounds weird, but once I found that, I felt a little bit more secure. It felt like a little piece of home. I felt like, OK, now I know where KFC is, and I have some people to chill with.

'There will be so many mixed people who have grown up outside of London who have a totally different experience, but where I was in my life meant that I had had zero exposure to that world, so it was really a lot to process.'

There is an assumption that being mixed provides you with chameleon-like powers of adaptability and assimilation. That we have a kind of beige camouflage that allows us to blend in anywhere. Offices, universities, all kinds of different institutions. We're supposed to be particularly adept at fitting in and adapting to different spaces thanks to the 'fluidity' of our identities, our lived experiences of multiple cultures, our ambiguous looks. This is what Jeanette was alluding to when she spoke about her ability to code-switch. But, as Bilal's experience shows, this isn't a universal power that applies to everyone with mixed heritage.

This ability to 'shift identities' and therefore exist comfortably in multiple spaces is frequently cited as a benefit of being mixed and spoken about as though it is something that all mixed people can access.[5] But it is more likely that this ability is dependent on individual personality types and the impact of your lived experiences. Jeanette was more likely to be able to switch more seamlessly between different contexts because she had experienced majority white and more ethnically diverse institutions growing up, whereas Bilal had not.

It may be that code-switching is a learnt behaviour, developed through existing in multiple spaces in which you are a minority, born from a desire to blend and to belong. Mixed people may be more likely to find themselves in spaces where they are different from everyone else – even within their own families – so they may have more opportunity to learn this skill. But it isn't some inherent superpower that mixed people are born with. We have to constantly work at our ability to blend, to fit in, and it can be exhausting.

★

I'm sweating. I can feel the tell-tale pinpricks tickling my armpits and I adjust my position slightly, tugging at the sleeves of my tailored, khaki boilersuit. I suspect I've worn the wrong outfit, and now all I can think about is whether the dark patches blooming

5  Jordan Soliz, Sierra, Gretchen Bergquist, Audra K. Nuru, Christine E. Rittenour, 'Perceived Benefits and Challenges of a Multiethnic Racial Identity: Insight From Adults With Mixed Heritage', Identity, Vol. 17, Issue 4, October 2017

beneath my arms are visible and whether or not my earrings – depicting an abstract naked female body – are completely inappropriate. But before I can snatch them out of my ears, a balding man in a pale pink shirt that strains against his stomach appears in my field of vision and says my name as a question.

I suddenly remember where I am – a job interview at a national media company. A big one. I silently curse myself for spending these last few precious moments of freedom worrying about the superficial rather than drilling my answers, anecdotes and examples one last time. I follow pink-shirt man down a wide, bright hallway, telling him about my dull journey across London in painstaking detail to fill the silence. The furnishings in the corridor are modern and minimal, the lights are bright. I trot slightly behind pink-shirt and try to rein in my inane small talk.

To get to this moment I had essentially been headhunted. I was asked to interview without having to formally apply because a new senior team member had read my work and wanted to consider me for their new team, something that was both incredibly flattering and wildly stress-inducing. This job interview felt like it was mine to fuck up. But I was prepared, and I was ready to swallow my imposter syndrome for the next hour and dazzle.

Pink-shirt leads me into a small office, a room almost entirely overwhelmed by a giant oak table. Another man in a light blue shirt is sitting on the far side of the table, waiting for us, papers laid out in front of him, pen in hand. He's older, and with a full head of perfectly white hair, he almost looks like pink-shirt's dad. I suppose he might be. I sit opposite the pair of them and feel a perfect bead of sweat roll down the inside of my upper arm like a droplet of dew. I ignore it. It's show time.

There's a feeling when you're tanking an interview and there's a feeling when you're nailing one. You just know. This interview feels like the latter. I'm light and conversational, confident, my examples of previous work spring from my brain at the slightest prompt, my ideas are met with appreciative nods, they laugh at a particularly lame joke. I'm impressing them, and my nerves – along with most of my sweat – have evaporated. But then something shifts.

I pitch an idea about racism in grassroots sport, specifically in women's sport. I explain why I think it's a topic that needs further investigation, where I would start, why it's important. But as I warm to my theme, I feel the temperature in the room drop. The nodding stops. I become instantly and acutely aware that I'm sat at a table with two middle-aged white men trying to explain why working to uncover institutional racism is a valid thing to do, and they both look incredibly awkward. I keep going but it's clear neither of them is sure where to take the conversation next.

'Is that . . . is that something you've experienced before?' the younger man in the pink shirt asks me without looking up from his papers.

'Racism? In . . . sport you mean?' I ask.

'Well, no, just . . . just in your life,' he says. Still not looking at me. Blue-shirt isn't looking at me either. My eyes flit between them as I desperately try to work out exactly what I'm being asked.

Have I ever experienced racism in my life? Is that what he's asking me? How on earth am I meant to answer that? And why on earth is it relevant? Later, I will conclude that this question is akin to being asked if I have ever experienced sexual harassment.. Unthinkably inappropriate for a professional interview. But I don't think that then. Not yet.

I'm still in interview mode. Ask me a question and I will answer. So, I stammer my way through some kind of response; trying to explain my experiences as a non-white woman to two white men, trying to prove that racism is real without triggering their fragility. I'm performing a complicated waltz through a minefield. Suddenly I'm talking about microaggressions, code-switching and painful, personal memories, when all I had wanted to do was lay out my content ideas and talk about women's sport. But I plough on because it doesn't feel like there's any other choice.

'I mean . . . I guess, yeah, sometimes in the workplace it can be difficult when you're a minority. I find I've often been the only non-white person in meetings before, and it can put you on the back foot . . . It feels like you're not always . . . listened to,' I manage, haltingly. Neither of them looks at me. None of us wants to be having this conversation.

'But that's not about *race*, is it?' says Blue-shirt, the older man. 'That's just because you're young.'

Now he looks at me, he locks his eyes on me. Pink-shirt doesn't look up from his papers. One of their phones vibrates against the table. There's a burst of laughter from someone passing in the corridor.

I feel the fight leave me. It rushes out of me all at once until I sag, deflated. My interview-ready urge to dazzle dissolves and I feel myself shrink. I can't continue to explain this to them. To prove that my lived experiences are true and valid.

'Oh right, maybe. It's probably that, yeah,' I say. Blue-shirt is still looking at me intently; he almost smirks as I concede defeat. Or maybe I imagine that. Pink-shirt still doesn't look up.

Then it's over and I'm out of the room. I close the door with a slightly trembling hand, my pulse roaring in my ears, my heart a hummingbird behind my ribs.

I burst out onto the street, it's January and the sky hangs low and heavy, kissing the wet concrete of the city. I push my way through grey throngs of Londoners and call the important names in my contacts list. I relay my story, still questioning why I feel upset, why I feel angry. Should I feel upset? Did anything even happen? It still doesn't hit me immediately. The injustice of the whole thing. The impossibility of that scenario.

Bafflingly, a few days later I got a call to tell me I had made it to the second round of interviews, but I declined and withdrew from the recruitment process. I spoke to someone there and suggested that Pink-shirt and Blue-shirt were spoken to about how they conduct their interviews. I don't know if this ever happened and I didn't make a formal complaint. I can't imagine either of them gave a second thought to that interview after I closed the door with my trembling hand. But it sat with me for weeks.

It's the self-doubt that makes these kinds of situations all the more unpleasant. The sneaky, underhand nature of these microaggressions that makes you uncertain, makes you tear yourself apart for the way you reacted or didn't react. They have an infuriating way of turning the scrutiny inwards. Rather than feeling empowered to call out problematic remarks, you're left grappling to decipher the real meaning and judging the tone of your response – all within a split second.

So much of my anger in the days after this interview was directed towards myself. I *allowed* them to put me in that position, I didn't dole out a sardonic dressing-down when they asked me about my experiences of racism; I sat there and smiled and tried to answer. But that is the entire point. That feeling of power-lessness is exactly the intention of microaggressions like these.

I didn't include this delightful memory because I think it's an experience that's unique to being mixed – what went on in that interview room happened because I'm not white. That was what the two interviewers saw; it didn't matter if I was mixed, Black, South Asian, or anything else – what mattered was the fact that I was *other*. However, I do wonder whether incidents like this take on a different dynamic due to my proximity to whiteness. If I was visibly, unequivocally Black, rather than mixed, would I have been questioned in the same way about my experiences of racism? Would I have been doubted with as much conviction? Of course, monoracial minorities – especially Black women – have their experiences of racism downplayed, delegitimised and scrutinised all the time – but I wonder if the fact that I am mixed gave blue-shirt more of a green light to push me on this in such a formal setting.

It's hard to know. But this kind of scrutiny and undermining is something that George has also experienced explicitly on a number of occasions. George is in his late twenties and he has a white mother and an Indian father (in the last chapter he explained his complex experience of passing as white), and, at the time we spoke, he worked as a communications and media officer at Kick It Out, the anti-discrimination in football organisation, but he has since taken on a new role at a different charity.

George says it can be tricky trying to talk passionately about racism and discrimination when people assume that you're white.

'It's rarely explicit, but particularly when I first started out and people didn't know me, I could just see people looking at me and thinking, "Oh, it's just another white guy who's jumping on the bandwagon",' he told me. I first met George in person about a year before this conversation and instantly loved talking to him about his experiences. He's compelling and articulate in a way that you might expect from a communications professional.

'It felt like they thought I was trying to profit off this issue in some way. It was always hard to define because no one ever directly said, "Well, you're white, what do you know?" – it was more subtle, like a feeling. There would be certain conversations I would be having, and I would find that some people just wouldn't really engage with me. They would nod and move on, and I can tell it's because they assume I don't have the right to talk about these issues.'

Even when people get to know him and find out that he is in fact mixed, George sometimes senses an air of lingering suspicion. He gets the feeling that people think he is trying to claim an ethnicity that doesn't really belong to him, that maybe he has an Indian great-grandparent, or great-uncle – rather than his own father.

But is there any grain of truth in these suspicions? Not in the suspicion that George isn't as Indian as he says he is, but whether he has the right to speak in these spaces looking the way he does. George is the first to acknowledge the immense privilege he possesses because of his appearance. Employers see him as a white man, and he knows this removes certain barriers for him and opens certain doors. He moves through public and professional spaces with an ease that people who are visibly 'other' will never know. However, he doesn't think it's fair to treat him as though he has zero understanding of what it's like to be an ethnic minority in this country. George has watched his father and brother face explicit racial abuse – in the street, at airports, from hostile neighbours – his entire life. He has even faced explicit racism himself, which takes on an unsettling quality when he explains that people have to know him quite well, and know that he's mixed, in order to be racist to him.

In his role at Kick It Out, George did vitally important work fighting racial discrimination and abuse in football, from professional leagues to the grassroots level. When Italian football league Serie A used artwork featuring monkeys in a bafflingly misguided 'anti-racism' campaign in December 2019, George did thirteen interviews for the BBC on behalf of Kick It Out in just one day, condemning the move and explaining how damaging it could be for Black players and fans. Talking to George, it was overwhelmingly apparent how passionate he is about promoting anti-racism, so it's easy to see why he gets frustrated when he is questioned on his authenticity.

In the aftermath of the Serie A scandal, George shared the interviews on Twitter and reiterated Kick It Out's stance on the story. A sports coach – a woman of colour – replied to the tweet, suggesting that George shouldn't be talking about racism having 'never experienced it', that he could 'never truly understand' what victims of racism go through.

This incident happened just days before I spoke to George, and I could tell it had upset him. When people make the incorrect assumption that he is not a minority in this country because of how he looks, it's always hard, but to be attacked about this when he was just trying to do his job was a step too far for George. The interviews weren't about his personal experience, so even though it was wrong for the coach to suggest he had no understanding of racism at all, George was actually being interviewed as an experienced Kick It Out spokesperson – he had every right to be doing them.

'First of all, I think those comments are just counterproductive to the real issue at hand,' George said. 'But then when you unpack it, the comments she made about me were actually problematic because of all the unfounded assumptions.'

George replied, letting the coach know that her claims

about him were wrong and that he is in fact mixed, with Indian heritage. She sent him a direct message in response, doubling down on her comments, telling him she already knew he was mixed, that it didn't change her opinion. It's this kind of response that George struggles with, particularly in a professional setting. He ends up trying to overcompensate, to justify his position, to find ways of working the fact that he's mixed into conversation early on to try to limit any hostility, which can, obviously, feel awkward.

'I want people to understand that I do have personal experience of racism and discrimination due to my background – that I'm not just someone wading into the equality sphere without any kind of prior knowledge,' he added.

'Maybe I shouldn't have to do that, but at the same time I understand that when people look at me, on face value alone they would assume that I have no personal experience. How would they know if they haven't spoken to me or know about my family?'

George gets it. He knows how the rest of the world sees him, and he doesn't mind putting in the extra legwork to explain his background, but what he can't understand is when people persist in their hostility and suspicion towards him, even after he's told them that he's mixed – like what happened with the sports coach on Twitter.

'The other week I was at an event and a woman was making a comment about white people generally in regard to racism – a completely valid comment – and she turned and said to me, "Oh sorry, no offence," before she said what she was going to say. I don't want to be lumped into that category because that's not who I am and that's not my experience,' he said. 'But I can understand why she did that. I had only just met her. How could she know any different? So that kind of thing doesn't get to me, I can take that.

'The problem comes when people *do* know, but continue to call me white, or treat me white anyway. I did sometimes wonder – working specifically in the field I do – if it wouldn't be easier in *some* ways if my heritage was more obviously visible, if I looked more clearly mixed.'

George's job is one of the only roles I've encountered where white privilege can work *against* you. But George caveats this by saying he knows this is the only situation where looking more Indian could be helpful, and is careful not to minimise the struggles faced by more visibly 'other' minorities in the UK.

One similarity I noticed between George and Jeanette is their generosity; their willingness to have the awkward conversations, to explain their position, to lay everything on the table to help people understand each other better. They both believe that silence, unease and tiptoeing around the issue of race is damaging minorities in the workplace and making it harder for them to be heard. It's a tricky one because why should the burden of explanation fall solely on the shoulders of minorities when Google exists? Jeanette admits that it can feel like a Catch-22 at times, that sometimes she wants nothing more than to tell people where to go, but she's patient and empathetic and that usually overrides her frustration.

'When I get the "What are you?" questions, or silly questions about my hair or my eyes, do I just shut somebody down and be like, "No, you don't get to ask me about these things."? That doesn't feel like the best way to handle it,' she told me.

'I try to talk to people about this stuff. I think that's so important, particularly in the workplace because it's just not helpful for people to feel like they can't ask questions or can't learn. We have to be able to talk about race at work in an open and honest way. It's the only way to break down the barriers and the unspoken bias.'

Jeanette thinks there's more than one benefit that comes from honesty in the workplace. From a personal perspective, she has found that not being afraid to speak her mind has helped her career; that being a bit of a loudmouth can be a good thing.

'Having an opinion is worth so much. I have this intense need to say what's right and wrong, always, regardless of the situation I'm in. Which could be to my detriment. But I think as long as you're doing it in a *constructive* way and you're not just poking holes, I think that's a good thing to do.'

She admits, though, that it can be a risky strategy. Speaking your mind as a woman of colour in the workplace is a dangerous game, one that can easily backfire. She knows that some people already see her as overly critical and 'difficult' by virtue of the fact that she isn't white, and that isn't something that's mitigated by the fact that she happens to be mixed. That's not what her white colleagues see when they look at her.

'There are some people in the workplace who can get away with murder, I see that,' said Jeanette. 'But that's not my experience, so I can only work with what I know and with how people respond to me. The moment you're on the spectrum "of colour", it doesn't matter where you fall on that spectrum, you're just non-white. And that's all that matters.

'That's one lesson my dad taught me early on in my life. Nobody is looking at my Filipino mum and thinking that she's white, no matter how light she is. There are some clear cases where the shade of your skin and where you fall on the spectrum of non-white does impact how you're treated, but not when it comes to majority-white workplaces. Other is other.'

Working environments will only become less hostile for minorities when managers, CEOs and anyone who holds power is able to find the language to effectively and productively talk about race, discrimination and bias. Using mixed employees to tick a diversity box because we're less 'threatening' and closer to what employees recognise in themselves is not the way to do it. Nor is slapping a light brown face on a poster to signal inclusivity, while denying those same faces a voice in meetings.

It's crucial that we're heard as well as seen, and the only way to do that is to have the uncomfortable conversations. Jeanette is ready to have them; George is ready to have them; Bilal's entire job is to start those conversations. And those of us who possess that door-opening 'palatability' must use this privilege to wedge the door open for others where we can. Because I want to see kids like those talented teenagers from Lewisham (who I did talk to in the end) taking their seats at the table in the not-too-distant future.

# Chapter 8

# The Future

When George Floyd died after a police officer knelt on his neck for eight minutes and 46 seconds, he became the latest name on a long list of Black police brutality victims. But it was different this time. He was more than a fleeting hashtag, more than an opportunity for performative online outrage. George Floyd's death triggered a reaction stronger than anything I have seen in my lifetime. Watching the video – or the snippets that I could bear – I felt a visceral anger that bubbled and rose like nausea, and it spilled out. I saw that same sick rage reverberating through everyone around me, my friends, my family, protesters around the country and globally.

It felt like a catalyst; the start of real, meaningful change. A desperate cry for equality that was finally being heard. I felt hopeful that this would be the moment, the turning point towards real justice, the start of something better.

Maybe it was the culmination of the stresses and tragedies that came with 2020 – the pressure-cooker effect of a seemingly endless global lockdown and loss on a scale we haven't seen for two generations – but the video of the harrowing final minutes of George Floyd's life seemed to collectively break something in all of us. Why was this the tipping point for a generation that has grown up with the internet? People who might have already seen videos of extreme violence, shootings, bombings; who have even, on some level, become used to seeing videos of unarmed Black suspects being beaten or killed by police officers? Whether it was borne of lockdown boredom, frustration, the fact that we all had more time on our hands, or simply the final straw that broke the camel's back, we all decided, simultaneously, that we had had enough. It could be that a year of 'unprecedented' events warranted an 'unprecedented' reaction, and it was long overdue.

We marched in our thousands, stopping traffic and grinding cities to a halt across the world. We gathered and chanted and waved banners and hung them from our rooftops, we wrote articles, letters, petitions, books, and raised millions for anti-racist organisations. Celebrities and influencers took up the cause, businesses and corporations swore to make positive changes, they apologised for previous actions, removed racist logos and culturally insensitive branding, they pledged to focus on 'diversity'. We tore down antiquated statues of racists and tossed them into the river. As symbols go, it doesn't get much more powerful than the satisfying splash as the weighty monument to a brutal slave owner connects with the surface of the water.

We promised to never stop talking about it. And then, almost immediately, everyone stopped talking about it. Not *everyone*, of course, but the swirling hurricane of outrage and unrest quickly died down to little more than a persistent breeze. The news cycle moved onto catchier stories, sexier injustices. The marches slowed and shrank. Our social media feeds returned to beaches and brunches, selfies and sunsets. You had to scroll to find a black square or a BLM hashtag. The allies got tired.

Looking back, this dying down and shift of focus was inevitable; people can't maintain that level of collective anger and momentum for long. But to see something that felt, to me at least, so ferocious, so incendiary, quelled to a flicker in a matter of weeks, was a shock. How could a movement that felt so urgent and extraordinary not turn out to be a significant and instant catalyst for change?

This moment in time did achieve something, however. Changes have been made, new perspectives have been forged, different voices have been heard. I'm not so naïve to believe that fundamental, systemic change can happen overnight, or in the space of a few months or a year, but the long-term changes are so much slower and more incremental than the velocity of actually living through these moments suggests. It feels like baby steps of progress, an almost imperceptible inching towards a different world, rather than the determined, infallible march I had hoped it would be. But even if the steps have to be tiny and slow, I am determined to keep taking them, to keep inching forward. Whatever the pace, at least we are finally heading in the right direction.

Weeks before my dad died – in the blissful three-month period where none of us knew that the cancer we thought had been successfully removed was actually running rampant through his body – I asked him about the Black Lives Matter movement. We had spoken about race and racism increasingly over the last few years, thanks in part to the work I do, my writing, but also because of my desire to know what he had experienced as a Black man growing up on a council estate with a white foster mum; in his professional life; in his personal life with my mum on his arm.

Dad never took anything too seriously, least of all himself, and issues of politics would usually raise little more than a shrug and a shake of the head. But racism was different. He wasn't apathetic, but he was disillusioned, and sometimes angry.

Which is why I didn't understand why he was less enthused by the images of the BLM protests on the news. He smiled and let me rant at length about the need for change, I sent him articles I had written about the urgency of this moment and he read every one, but he was non-committal when I asked his opinion.

'This is different though, Dad, this feels different,' I said to him.

'This feels different *for you*,' he replied. And we returned to a topic he found much more interesting – which movies he had watched that week and which ones I had to add to my watchlist. Dad always preferred to engage with politics and injustice in fictional, cinematic form, a symptom of thirty years spent working in news.

Soon after Dad died, my mum told me a story that helped me understand why he felt like this. Why he wasn't convinced that this was a pivotal moment for Black lives.

In 1992, my parents went to stay with Dad's biological mum, Pauline, carting three-year-old me and one-year-old Becky along with them. Pauline was living in Greenford, Middlesex; this was a few years before she moved back home and gained her official title of 'Nana-in-Jamaica', which is how Becky and I would come to refer to her once were both old enough to talk.

It was April or May, so our visit fell during the weeks when Los Angeles was burning with unbridled anger and violence following the death of Rodney King and the acquittal of the four police officers suspected of causing his death. My sister and I were sleeping, but my parents and Pauline were glued to the news, watching protestors set buildings on fire, loot shops, smash up cars and hurl rocks at the riot police. Sixty-three people died in the violence. My parents watched wide-eyed as the uprising unfolded – they had never seen anything like it in their lifetimes.

To their astonishment, Pauline, a woman who prided herself

on being prim, proper and respectable, a woman who spoke exclusively in a regal received pronunciation, as though the Queen might be listening, suddenly slipped into the strongest Jamaican accent and yelled at the TV: 'They should burn it all down!' My parents just looked at each other.

Surely this was the moment *everything* would change. How could anything go back to normal after such a widespread display of visceral anger and disruption? How could racial injustice persist when the people had risen up and fought back with such vehement determination? How could anything slip back to what it was before?

But here we are, thirty years later, marching about the same shit. And in the months since those global Black Lives Matter marches, the BBC allowed a white reporter to say the N-word in a news report; Black students have had their futures derailed as teachers' biases impacted exam results; a police officer in Wisconsin shot Jacob Blake in the back seven times. Our moment of change is yet to materialise.

Perhaps thirty years from now, my daughter will tell me how everything is going to be different this time, and I will remember George Floyd, smile, and change the subject. But I'm not ready to change the subject yet.

How we talk about mixedness is a crucially important element in the wider conversation about race, racial hierarchies, and whose lives matter. As a Black and mixed woman, I have felt this urgently over the last year. We need to find a language and a narrative about the mixed population that doesn't oversimplify, that doesn't reduce us to a monolithic group, that neither vilifies nor celebrates us for the simple fact of our mixedness. This is bigger than our individual feelings, too. We don't *only* want to improve this conversation because it would be nice for mixed people to feel seen and understood and not reduced to stereotypes (although this is important too); upholding these simplistic and flawed perspectives about mixedness is actually deeply damaging to the wider understanding of racial equality and the social constructions of race.

The mixed population is growing. There are more people with mixed heritage being born in the UK than ever before, so it is vital that we find a way to bring more nuance, history and research into the conversation about mixedness. The negative and problematic stereotypes and beliefs about the mixed population that still persist today are bolstering damaging understandings of 'race' and reinforcing hierarchical structures that celebrate whiteness above all else and continue to oppress minoritised communities. Reframing how we think about mixedness and how we talk about mixed identity is crucial in dismantling these archaic systems, in dismantling white supremacy.

I'm sorry to bring it back to Meghan Markle again, but I have to. When her son Archie was born, the media lost it. Even while he was still in the womb there was speculation about what he would look like, how 'mixed' he would look, how 'Black' he would look, the role he would play in future 'race relations' for the country; the pressure on him to become some kind of progressive symbol of racial unity began before he could even utter his first word or hold up his own head.

The day after the Royal youngster was born, Black writer and broadcaster Trevor Phillips wrote a letter to Archie that was published in the *Daily Mail*. He said that Archie would have the 'responsibility to be a bridge between white Britain and Black Britain on [his] shoulders'.[1]

---

1 Trevor Phillips, 'A poster boy for a brave new Britain: Equalities guru TREVOR PHILLIPS says why the first ever mixed-race royal can make us all proud', Daily Mail, 6th May, 2019

In the letter which, bizarrely, addresses the newborn directly, Phillips goes on to say: 'Every time we look at you, we will see a symbol of an institution that has been willing to adapt, not just for its own sake, but in order to reflect change in our nation.'

There are a number of things I dislike about this letter but calling a one-day-old mixed baby a 'bridge' between two worlds is definitely high on the list. Not only is it overly simplistic to imply that the mere presence of a child with Black heritage in the Royal Family will have any ability to unpick generations of excusive elitism – that his cherubic brown face will miraculously change the hearts and minds of racists up and down the country – but it also robs baby Archie of his autonomy. Deciding that Archie is the 'bridge', the key to improving racial equity simply by existing, is hopelessly idealistic, but it's also a really unfair position to put a child in. He doesn't get a say in this, and no one seems interested in what he will have to say when he is old enough. The simple fact of his existence and how he looks is enough for everyone else to define his position in the world for him.

Being born into an unfathomable amount of expectation and a rigid, preordained path is, admittedly, normal for Royal babies, but the scrutiny that Archie faced from day one was something different. Is it any wonder his parents decided to ditch the whole system, sue the British press, and let their little boy grow up in a different country instead?

This idea of Archie as a 'symbol' is exactly the thinking behind the theory of a 'golden generation' who are human-ity's last hope for change. But, as I have already discussed, it is inherently problematic to think of a hugely varied and diverse group of people as collectively 'symbolic' of anything. The interviews alone in this book show how wildly different the mixed experience can be depending on age, class, where you live, your specific mix of heritages, and so many other factors. So, how can the mixed population as a whole represent a singular message?

Put simply, we can't, of course we can't. But this symbolism is repeatedly pushed on us, stripping us of our individuality, our opinions, our voices. Symbols are visual, aesthetic and, crucially, silent. Using mixed people as a symbolic hope for an exciting, multicultural future is an easy win for white people who want to seem progressive, without doing any work to examine their own culpability in the inequalities of racial hierarchies.

Most of these people – the people who like the 'symbolism' of mixedness – will believe that their effusive approval of interracial marriages and the growing mixed population is a badge of liberal honour. That it proves how open, accepting and fair they are. However, it is rarely mentioned that celebrating the mixed population is intricately linked to a proximity to whiteness. These discussions are rarely inclusive of people who are mixed without whiteness, or those who have darker skin and more distinctly 'other' features. Maybe the theory of a 'golden generation' isn't even a celebration of mixedness, but a celebration of other races slowly becoming more palatable to white people.

So, how do we talk about the future then? The fact is that the mixed population *is* growing in the UK, and that trajectory is unlikely to change. This isn't necessarily a cause for celebration, but it does mean that we need to find better ways to talk about race, better ways of conceptualising identity beyond the binaries of Black and white, better ways to make space for alternative narratives.

When we look back over the stories that have been shared in this book (Anna grappling with the privileges that come with passing as white, Alexander unpacking the fetishisation and objectification he faces on the dating scene, Jeanette struggling to belong to mixedness as a dark-skinned woman without white heritage), the standout feature is the individuality of these experiences. It couldn't be clearer that the mixed experience is not a singular one. There is no *one* narrative, no *one* story that can sum up what it means to be mixed. We need to move away from conversations that assume we are a homogenous group. They are reductive, exclusive, and actually help to reinforce the negative biases and stereotypes that have existed for decades.

It's also important to remember that the way we speak about mixedness in terms of contemporary thinking isn't necessarily as positive as it might first appear. The recent popularisation of mixedness – reinforced by the disproportionate focus on mixed beauty and the rise of racial ambiguity as an aesthetic trend on social media – isn't the progressive step forward that it might seem on the surface.

I understand how it sounds to complain about the fact that mixed people like me are fetishised for our 'beauty' and 'exoticism', for being assumed to have the 'best of both worlds'. A lot of the complicated microaggressions that mixed people have to deal with are worlds apart from the overtly damaging and negative forms of racism that darker-skinned minorities – specifically Black people, even more specifically Black *women* – face on a daily basis. The two things are non-comparable. It isn't helpful or accurate to equate being hypersexualised with being demonised, being told that your racialised features make you *more* attractive to being told they make you *unattractive*. But that shouldn't mean there isn't also space to discuss the different forms of racism that mixed people experience. We definitely have the range to do both.

I have already unpicked the problematic nature of the kinds of 'compliments' mixed people are expected to be grateful for, but you really can't understate the dangers of excessively celebrating the attributes of mixed individuals and positioning us as in some way 'exceptional'. Whether the end result is positive or negative, assigning specific talents and attributes to the entire mixed population is based on the same discredited racial pseudo-science of the past; in saying that mixed people are more beautiful, more talented, more likely to succeed, you are only a hair's breadth away from concluding the opposite, which is where we have been before. It is unsettling to see this kind of thinking creeping back into the mainstream.

'Whilst it might be tempting to see such imaginings as positive pronouncements of mixedness,' explained Caballero and Aspinall in the final chapter of their book, 'the other side of the "hybrid vigour" coin is hybrid degeneracy.

'The nineteenth century arguments that racial mixing produced weaker offspring and threatened society as a whole versus the claim that it enhanced and strengthened races were both born of the same pseudo-scientific framework that the races were biologically, physically and intellectually inherently different. Replacing arguments over the degenerative qualities of mixedness by those asserting the strength of hybrid vigour continues the pathological framework.'[2]

So, we are right to be suspicious about these dubious 'compliments', these unsettling assertions that we are especially beautiful, 'better' in some vague way, or that we are the key to a utopian future? When people say things like this it leaves a cold feeling in my stomach that is hard to define and even

2  Chamion Caballero and Peter J. Aspinall, 'Mixed Race Britain in the Twentieth Century', Palgrave Macmillan, London, 2018

harder to call out – how can I get angry at someone for saying something that sounds like a compliment? But we are right to be attuned to this, to call it out where we can, to explain whenever we can why it's problematic.

Another issue that needs to be overcome is the tendency for people to lump mixed individuals together as though we are all one. As though everyone with mixed heritage has a singular experience, a singular place in the world. Whether the assumptions about us are seemingly positive or negative, that we are confused, pitiable, not enough of one thing or another, the thing that really grates is the idea that any of these assumptions apply to *all* of us. The mixed population is kaleidoscopic. We are multifaceted, complicated, unique and every one of us experiences the world differently. Yes, there are commonalities that thread through the mixed experience, things that connect us and help us relate to each other in ways that non-mixed people cannot, but our individuality is our strength.

Homogenising minority groups and stripping them of individual identity is a tried-and-tested technique that maintains the unequal balance of power. You'll notice that white people are rarely talked about in terms of a collective; it is their privilege to be viewed as individuals with their own thoughts, beliefs and motivations. Minority groups are denied this level of autonomy and consistently categorised collectively as 'something else': BAME, POC, 'other'.

The way to push back against this homogenisation is to insist on our own definitions, to define our identity on our own terms rather than by how we are perceived by others, to realise that who we are is shaped by our individual experiences of life that no one else has been through (even if they happen to look similar), to create the space for more categories, for alternative narratives, to rail against the binary understanding of ethnicity that tries to squeeze us into one box or another, to find our freedom in those in between spaces, to reject the boxes entirely.

Inevitably, we have arrived back at identity again: who we are and who we feel ourselves to be versus how the rest of the world sees us. So much of the contemporary conversation about mixedness ends up cycling endlessly around issues of identity; how it feels on an individual basis to be mixed. I focus on it a lot in this book – there's a whole chapter on it. And it is definitely a necessary part of the conversation. In a world where identity, particularly in terms of ethnicity, is still so limited, poorly communicated and narrow in its definitions, it makes sense for people who fall outside of those pre-existing categories to feel conflicted about where they belong. Most mixed people will hit a point in their lives where they ask themselves, 'Where do I fit?'. We need to have these conversations. I certainly did, and I'm sure I will hit moments in my life again where I feel that old flare-up of uncertainty and lack of belonging.

Talking about identity helps with this. It helps us to realise that we're not alone with these feelings, that we are not isolated, that we are justified in what we feel, and that we're not imagining it. Belonging to something that is bigger than yourself helps you feel grounded in the world, helps you feel anchored, safe and supported. This is why discussions about identity matter, and why identity politics is a vital part of modern social interactions that shouldn't be sneered at or derided.

It's also important though that we aren't *only* talking about identity, or talking about it in a vacuum. Conversations about identity are only helpful or accurate when they are looked at in context. There is no point in discussing what it means to be mixed without acknowledging where that mixedness is positioned: where you grew up, what point in time you were born, your socioeconomic place in the world, your specific heritage mix. Without these contextual markers of real-world relevance, discussions of identity for identity's sake become meaningless and can even feed into outdated, unhelpful stereotypes.

Sociology student and podcast host Chantelle Lewis wrote in a 2019 blog post that these discussions 'often position identity in abstraction from discussions of place and space, class, gender, and wider structural issues'.[3]

She warns against the cyclical nature of discussing identity without also acknowledging the privileges that many mixed people experience and the complexities of proximity to whiteness.

'There has [been] and should continue to be space to discuss how mixedness is narrated and lived within families, places and institutions, but the conversation needs to broaden. We can talk about these complex issues whilst also addressing the privileges we are afforded which in turn are often determined by social networks but importantly, place and space.'

She adds: 'We need to be thinking a lot harder about how we communicate these issues and how they should be attentive to intersectional specificities.'

Chantelle's PhD research aims to grapple with the 'difficulties' of mixedness and move the conversation on from identity by talking about being mixed in relation to racism, class, patriarchy and colourism. There is more to who we are than endless discussions about who we *feel* we are.

Being mixed means constantly explaining yourself: why you

---

3   Chantelle Lewis, 'Please can we stop talking about "mixed-race" identity (on its own)?', Discover Society, 23rd July, 2019

look the way you do, why you identify the way you do, why you act the way you do. It can be exhausting to have these answers demanded of you, particularly if you are still grappling with the complexity of these questions yourself. Many of us exist in fluidity; how we are perceived changes depending on where we are and who we are with. We flip between facing discrimination and experiencing privilege; some doors slam in our faces while other doors are opened for us. Our access to privilege is usually completely out of our hands, which can feel disempowering and unsettling.

On the other side of the coin, being mixed can be a joyful, positive, powerful experience. So many of the people I have interviewed in this book are a testament to that. I think about Bilal learning to connect with the Asian side of his family through food and traditions; I think about Aziza embracing her darker skin tone and hair texture to teach her little sister there are more ways to be beautiful; I think of Mel at her wedding surrounded by vibrancy, love and a plethora of diversity, tears in her eyes at the beauty of it all.

Our experiences, both positive and negative, are unique and deeply varied. There are stories of unity, of strength, of discovery and pride in heritage, of acceptance, of deeper understanding. There is a blending of traditions; a joy in creating new traditions; there is a celebration of the food, the music, the clothes and the folklore that builds our individual histories, our individual narratives. There is so much joy in our individuality, and so much power in our inability to fit into society's prescribed little boxes.

Historically, it has always been presented as a great tragedy that mixed people can't be neatly categorised, that we don't have an official box to belong to in terms of race. We have been repeatedly portrayed as lost, confused, rejected, unmoored.

And in the past, many of us will have experienced these things, but not because we don't sit in a singular racial category. It happens because of how other people react to our multiplicity, because of an innate suspicion of anyone who deviates from the limited system of categorisation.

As I said at the beginning of the book, as a society we love putting people into boxes. We love to give people tidy and complete labels that define who they are and where they fit within our social systems. Every label that we attach to a person – from age, gender, sexual orientation to socioeconomic class – is ultimately a form of control, conformity, and a means to limit both potential and possibility in an individual. We have attached so much meaning to each label that to deviate from the expected behaviours from someone in your category is frequently pathologised, presented as a problem, an illness. To be mixed is to challenge the limited categories of race from the moment you are born. So it is no wonder that we have been subject to both stigmatisation and disproportionate celebration at different points in history.

Instead of a utopian future in which everyone is vaguely brown, and nobody sees colour, I would like a future where mixed Brits are no longer disempowered, no longer have their identities thrust upon them by others, and are given the space to explore and express the messy, untidy, contradictory lived experiences that are entirely unique to them. I want us to be neither celebrated nor denigrated, but free to exist as individuals with worth and value that is entirely separate to how the rest of the world happens to perceive our ethnicities.

When I look in the mirror, I see my dad in the sloping, slight imbalance of my eyebrows, the deep crinkles that form at the corners of my eyes when I laugh, my inability to not show off every single tooth when I smile. I feel his history within me, I carry his Blackness, and with it the strength and resilience that he built in the face of systemic inequalities. At the same time, I see my mum in the tip of my nose, the soft point of my chin, the cheekbones that give my face its angular quality. I carry her whiteness too; I feel it when I'm welcomed into certain circles, when I move with ease through spaces where Black women would be shut out.

But I feel them, both of them, so much deeper than that, deeper than how I look. Who they are informs everything that I am. I hear my mum's gentleness spilling from my own mouth, and her unexpected fire in the face of injustice; her understated bravery flows in my veins, too. I feel myself sitting in Dad's muted self-assurance, his humility and quiet confidence, his ability to back himself even when no one else would. The love that he left in this world courses through my blood and gives me so much strength. These aren't biological things that I have inherited through my genes, these are lessons my parents have taught me, attributes that I aspire to because of how they brought me up. And I have some control over how I channel this in myself. We all do.

None of us are able to control the physical attributes that we inherit from our parents, from the different elements of our histories. We can't control how our features will manifest physically, and how those features will be perceived and racialised by others. We can't control how 'mixed' we look, how 'other' we look. But we can control the lessons we learn from our multiple backgrounds, how we interpret our own stories, how we communicate that to others. We have the agency to claim our individual identities for ourselves. And that feels pretty damn empowering.

# Acknowledgments

To my dad – thank you for reading all of the bits of this book that I needed you to read. And for never leaving me in any doubt of how proud you were. To my mum and my little sister – thank you for being my life-support system during the hardest year of our lives.

To Jared – thank you for putting up with the many early mornings and weekends of writing, and for convincing me to believe in myself.

To Donna, Ria and Ryan – thank you for being the most brilliant sounding board. And to too many other friends to name who have cheered me endlessly through this process. You know who you are.

To my editor, Marleigh – thank you for loving and championing this idea, and for holding my hand through the sometimes scary process of writing my first book.

To my contributors, Luke, Joseph, Hannah, Ciaran, Annalisa, Becky, Mel, Alexander, Aziza, Laura, Bilal, Jeanette, George and Anna – thank you for trusting your stories with me.

# Credits

Natalie Morris and Trapeze would like to thank everyone at Orion who worked on the publication of *Mixed/Other*.

**Editorial**
Marleigh Price

**Copy editor**
Clare Wallis

**Proofreader**
Loma

**Audio**
Paul Stark
Amber Bates

**Contracts**
Anne Goddard
Paul Bulos
Jake Alderson

**Design**
Debbie Holmes
Joanna Ridley

Nick May

**Editorial Management**
Jane Hughes

**Finance**
Jasdip Nandra
Afeera Ahmed
Elizabeth Beaumont
Sue Baker

**Marketing**
Folayemi Adebayo

**Production**
Claire Keep

**Publicity**
Alainna Hadjigeorgiou
Patricia Deever

**Sales**
Jennifer Wilson
Esther Waters
Victoria Laws
Ellie Kyrke-Smith
Frances Doyle
Georgina Cutler

**Operations**
Jo Jacobs
Sharon Willis
Lisa Pryde
Lucy Brem

# Help us make the next generation of readers

We – both author and publisher – hope you enjoyed this book. We believe that you can become a reader at any time in your life, but we'd love your help to give the next generation a head start.

Did you know that 9 per cent of children don't have a book of their own in their home, rising to 13 per cent in disadvantaged families*? We'd like to try to change that by asking you to consider the role you could play in helping to build readers of the future.

We'd love you to think of sharing, borrowing, reading, buying or talking about a book with a child in your life and spreading the love of reading. We want to make sure the next generation continue to have access to books, wherever they come from.

And if you would like to consider donating to charities that help fund literacy projects, find out more at **www.literacytrust.org.uk** and **www.booktrust.org.uk**.

THANK YOU

*As reported by the National Literacy Trust